Humanities for Humans

Humanities for Humans

Clear Thinking on Challenging Issues

Edited by
Irene Kacandes

DE GRUYTER

ISBN 978-3-11-152852-6
e-ISBN (PDF) 978-3-11-153148-9
e-ISBN (EPUB) 978-3-11-153179-3
DOI https://doi.org/10.1515/9783111531489

This work is licensed under the Creative Commons Attribution-NonCommercial-NoDerivatives 4.0 International License. For details go to https://creativecommons.org/licenses/by-nc-nd/4.0/.

Creative Commons license terms for re-use do not apply to any content (such as graphs, figures, photos, excerpts, etc.) not original to the Open Access publication and further permission may be required from the rights holder. The obligation to research and clear permission lies solely with the party re-using the material.

Library of Congress Control Number: 2024951117

Bibliographic information published by the Deutsche Nationalbibliothek
The Deutsche Nationalbibliothek lists this publication in the Deutsche Nationalbibliografie; detailed bibliographic data are available on the internet at http://dnb.dnb.de.

© 2025 the author(s), editing © 2025 Irene Kacandes, published by Walter de Gruyter GmbH, Berlin/Boston, Genthiner Straße 13, 10785 Berlin
The book is published open access at www.degruyter.com.

Cover image: Humanities for Humans discussion, September 27, 2022. © 1014 – Space for Ideas. Photo: Roshni Khatri.
Typesetting: Integra Software Services Pvt. Ltd.

www.degruyter.com
Questions about General Product Safety Regulation:
productsafety@degruyterbrill.com

Contents

Note to Readers from the Editor —— VII

Sponsors' Foreword —— IX

Irene Kacandes
Introduction —— 1

Part One: **Naming the Problem**

Dagmar Herzog
Racism, Fascism, Eugenics: The Political Work of Consequential Fictions —— 31

Michael G. Hanchard
Racial Regimes, Here and Now —— 41

Kathryn Abrams
On the Agency of Migrants —— 55

Part Two: **Assessing the Stakes**

Bruce Robbins
Equality in (Our) Time —— 69

Robin D. G. Kelley
Humanities in the Face of Genocide —— 77

Rebecca Tsosie
Indigenous Sustainability and an Ethic of Place: Can We Protect the Lands that We Love? —— 91

Part Three: **Crafting Connection**

Harriet Hawkins
All Power to the Imagination —— 109

Liz Lerman and Martha Minow
Turning Controversy into Connection —— 119

Marianne Hirsch
Reparative Memory in Practice —— 141

Appendices

Appendix One —— 163

Appendix Two —— 165

Appendix Three —— 167

Note to Readers from the Editor

My strong hope is you decide that this is not quite like any other non-fiction book you may have picked up to read before. To be sure, it resembles most closely what is often called an "edited volume" or an "anthology," meaning that it's composed of essays by different academic authors centered on a theme. There are a variety of authors here, and they are sharing on subjects that could be grouped under "current concerns" or "hot button issues." These "challenging topics," as I refer to them in this book's subtitle, were originally featured in the conversation series between academics and aimed at the general public, curated and moderated by me, called "Humanities for Humans." However, what you'll find here are not just printed versions of those conversations – though to give you the flavor of them I do include a transcription of a long section of one – and neither are they formal academic essays in the form usually found in "edited volumes." In their tone and style, they are closer, rather, to something you might see on newspaper Op-Ed pages. Further differentiating this book from academic anthologies, you'll hear my voice punctually throughout. My intention in speaking up is to make this book as accessible and engaging as possible to a wide range of readers by breaking down the barrier between academic authors and general readers. I've already mentioned including my voice to that end, and you'll soon see that the authors speak about themselves using the word "I" – usually avoided in traditional academic writing. As here, my voice will be indicated with italics, which will make it easier for you to skip, if you find you prefer not to hear my thoughts before you formulate your own. Use of "we" comes up as a topic in several moments in this book, especially as a warning to exercise caution about who "we" think "we" speak for. I use "we" mainly to avoid taking credit for things that were done together and to create – I hope – a sense of journey with readers of this book. However, in the spirit of taking responsibility, I do signal that I am responsible for the shape of this book, and if you find mistakes here, they are probably mine.

Without further ado, here we go.

Sponsors' Foreword

The two individuals who drafted this foreword on behalf of the sponsors of the "Humanities for Humans" project are smart, energetic women I've had the privilege of interacting with for years in numerous contexts.

Manuela Gerlof and I met when she was put in charge of a book series I'd been involved in editing, "Interdisciplinary German Cultural Studies," for the publishing house De Gruyter in Berlin, Germany. Although Manuela's responsibilities at De Gruyter have increased dramatically over the years since our first acquaintance and she's no longer my direct contact, we've managed to stay in close touch. She has continued to be a wonderful resource for me in relation to that book series for which I still serve as the editor. Though I'll mostly let her tell this story, when the De Gruyter Foundation approached Manuela about supporting the Humanities in North America, she asked me what I thought about an idea for how to do so. That initial email led to the back-and-forth brainstorming that eventually led to refining my proposal for a conversation series, which in turn became more feasible and took on further specificity when I thought to put Manuela and the De Gruyter Foundation in contact with a non-profit organization in New York run by Katja Donovan.

Katja Donovan and I first met when I was serving as an officer of the German Studies Association, the largest organization in the world for the interdisciplinary study of all topics German. This designation refers not just to issues related to the nation Germany, but to other nations with German-speaking populations and to German-speaking groups and individuals. When the German government decided to repurpose rather than sell a lovely if code-violating building they owned on Fifth Avenue in New York City, Katja was hired as the first executive director to oversee what that building could become. She recruited me as a Board member for the project which Board members and staff collectively subsequently decided to name "1014. Space for Ideas" – the 1014 referring to the building's address and the Space for Ideas explaining its function. Having been inspired by the great events that Katja and her team were already sponsoring at 1014, I thought of her immediately when Manuela and I found our way to a conversation series.

The series "Humanities for Humans" has its roots in personal connections, cultivated – as many ideas are – through vibrant discussions spoken across the steam of hot beverages and with the conviction that there is value in thinking deeply and critically about difficult questions.

In the summer of 2022, the three of us – Irene, Katja, and Manuela – met for lunch at Café Einstein, only a short walk from De Gruyter's headquarters in Berlin Tiergarten. Manuela, then vice president of Humanities and Social Sciences publishing at De Gruyter, was nearing the start of what would become a two-year stay in Boston as part of an initiative to expand De Gruyter's network in North America. Irene, not only book series editor at De Gruyter but also board member at the New York-based not-for-profit 1014, had the idea for a conversation series and to connect the two organizations to help bring it to life. As executive director of 1014, Katja was thrilled about the idea of bringing her recently founded organization together with a publisher with a centuries-long history to join forces to foster trans-Atlantic perspectives. Soon, the three became not only collegial partners but also close friends.

Building on nearly three centuries of history and experience as an independent publisher of humanities works – from the Brothers Grimm, Immanuel Kant, and Friedrich Nietzsche to contemporary scholars working across all research fields – De Gruyter has demonstrated an unwavering commitment to the pursuit of knowledge. An integral component of this dedication comes from the De Gruyter Foundation, a nonprofit organization founded and endowed by the publisher to support scholars, particularly in the humanities and social sciences. Since 2006, the De Gruyter Foundation has funded more than one hundred projects, including prizes celebrating research excellence, book donations to university libraries, scholarships for individuals, and the digitization of important manuscripts and archives.

It didn't take long for us to recognize that the De Gruyter Foundation was a perfect match for 1014's mission to promote trans-Atlantic dialogue and creative thinking about some of the world's most complex challenges. The partnership that followed was a natural consequence of our mutual interests and desire to infuse academic debates with a personal touch while encouraging a positive and welcoming space for nuanced conversation.

"Humanities for Humans," our mutual conversation series, with both in-person and virtual episodes, immediately drew a large audience into 1014's space for ideas. Breaking down theoretical concepts and making complex ideas understandable and applicable to real life deeply resonated with our public audiences in Germany and the United States. At a time when our Western societies primarily focus on technological advances and scientific innovation, the series revealed the power of the Humanities in dealing with today's global challenges from climate change to migration, identity and intersectionality, reparation, and more. It inspired the creativity and imagination we need to contribute to essential debates and to collectively shape our future.

Two years later, the overwhelmingly positive feedback led us to the idea to publish the essence of some of the eight conversations in this volume. Unlike most edited volumes of scholarly work, this collection is designed to capture the dynamic feel of the live events and showcase the thoughts, ideas, and debates for a wider public audience. A critical component of this is the free, worldwide access to the digital publication as part of De Gruyter Brill's wider Open Access initiative, driving a sustainable future for sharing knowledge between academia and the public. The recorded events will also remain available on De Gruyter Brill's YouTube channel[1] as well as the 1014 website.[2] Plans are already in the works to continue the conversation series, and we couldn't be more excited for what comes next.

As sponsors and friends, we would like to express our deepest gratitude and admiration to Irene for her engagement as curator, moderator, and spirit of this project. Her vision and ability to bring scholars together who, like her, are undaunted by challenges and unafraid to take positions on complex sociocultural issues, has formed the heart of this project. A special thanks also goes out to the events and communications teams at 1014 as well as De Gruyter for their time and energy, not to mention the space, resources, and work to make these events possible, whether in person on Manhattan's Upper East Side or virtually across the globe. We also extend our heartfelt thanks to all the contributors and discussants, without whom neither the event series nor this book would have been possible. As a reader of this book, we are sure you will feel their passion and enthusiasm to change things for the better as they have undoubtedly permeated the pages ahead.

Katja Wiesbrock Donovan, Executive Director, 1014. Space for Ideas
Manuela Gerlof, Chief Publishing Officer, De Gruyter Brill

---

1 https://www.youtube.com/@DegruyterPublishers.
2 https://www.1014.nyc/humanities-for-humans (Website will change).

Irene Kacandes
Introduction

Having prodded the contributors to this book to step out of their comfort zones and write up a biographical sketch in the first person, I certainly have to complete that exercise myself. Here goes!

It was not my childhood dream to become a professor, though I did realize at an early age that I was good at school, and that I seemed to have a knack for helping others learn things. I am a middle child, third daughter of four who were eventually joined by two younger brothers, born to parents who grew up in Fascist-occupied Greece. I put it that way because my father was actually born in the U.S. to immigrant parents, whereas my mother was born and raised on the Cycladic island of Andros. They both survived World War II in Greece as children, and their war experiences became one thing they shared when they first met years later in Ithaca, New York. Mostly my father's war experiences became something that insidiously lurked in the background of my own otherwise peaceful middle-class girlhood in White Plains, a suburb of New York City.

My friend and contributor to this book, Marianne Hirsch, coined the term "postmemory" for the traumatic experiences of others dominating one's own psyche. When Marianne first explained postmemory to me in the mid-1990s, it made immediate sense and awakened specters that had haunted my childhood. Trauma, postmemory, and World War II became important topics I have explored in my academic work – among other places, in a book I published about my paternal family's wartime experiences and how the memory of them was stored in several generations. Titling it *Daddy's War. Greek American Stories* (2009), I labeled it a "paramemoir," because while it does recount some of my own experiences, it includes not only the experiences but also the voices of many others. Further differentiating it from standard memoir, I analyze stories told to me in terms of oral culture, historical truth, trauma, and personal identity markers like gender, age, and birth order, rendering this book "para" – "more." Paramemoir goes beyond memoir.

Another concept in that book and one that I suspect I somehow grasped from a young age is what I call "co-witnessing." Co-witnessing resembles postmemory and paramemoir in that all concern individuals' relationships to other people's trauma. A constitutive element of co-witnessing involves a conscious decision to learn and then pass on the traumatic experiences of others who perhaps cannot tell their own stories due to continuing traumatization or imprisonment or even death. Co-witnessing requires careful listening and often research, and the co-witness needs to be vigilant not to appropriate the experiences of the victim.

As for the "German" side of my career, I trace it gratefully to my wonderful high-school German teacher, Eldine von Burchard, who was not only a talented pedagogue, but who also went well beyond her required responsibilities. She planned, for instance, the very first exchange between our high school and one in Hamburg, Germany. I took to living with a German family and speaking only German like a duck to water – not an inappropriate metaphor given how much it rained that month of my first and happily not last trip to Germany and German-speaking places. Still, that German became a major part of my education and career is mostly due to good advice from my older sisters to major in a small field so that I wouldn't get lost at Harvard in the crowd of large majors like theirs. Though I loved English literature, my best chances to enter an honors program called "History and Literature" lay in the strategy of proposing German as my field. This worked. Not ignoring my original love of English and having discovered during college the academic study of Greece, I went on to a Ph.D. in Comparative Literature.

I've had the good fortune of teaching not only at excellent institutions – Harvard, the University of Texas, and for the longest part of my career at Dartmouth College – but also at ones that have allowed me to truly pursue my interests wherever they've taken me. Thus, the ten books I've authored or edited range in topic from orality in prose fiction to language pedagogy to teaching the representation of the Holocaust to new approaches to analyzing Eastern Europe to talking about death. I was recently asked how my religious faith inflects my academic work. I hope, but can't be sure, that it comes through in my commitment to justice by helping people desire and understand connection to one another.

And below begins what I want to share with you about the project "Humanities for Humans," of which this book constitutes a part.

For decades, I have begun my classes by commenting on the title I have given them and making sure that I and the students understand what our goals are. These are two of my goals for this introduction, too. An additional one is reporting on the conversation series "Humanities for Humans" as it unfolded from 2022–2024, with a fourth goal being an introduction to what readers will encounter in this book that does not constitute the talk series in another form.

"Humanities for Humans"?

The "humanities" element in the title could seem obvious for inclusion since the request from the project's initiating sponsor specified doing something to highlight the humanities fields in North America. The Walter de Gruyter Foundation after all is a foundation connected to De Gruyter Verlag (now De Gruyter Brill), an independent mid-size international publisher headquartered in Berlin, Germany. The publisher has a renowned program in humanities and social sciences and has been focusing its activities to increase the visibility of their program and the communities it serves in North America.

But what are the humanities, you might ask, especially if you're of a certain age, as I am, but did not make academic humanities your profession. In the first half of my career, admissions committees, first year advisors, and we professors often had to explain what the rubric of humanities covered when students arrived at college. I think that's not as mysterious to students or their parents nowadays as it used to be, due to the proliferation of humanities curricula at the high school and even elementary levels. I recently found this explanation of the "humanities block" of the fourth-grade curriculum on the website of the Ramsey, New Jersey school district: "Reading, Writing, and Social Studies units are intentionally aligned around one big idea/theme and a few essential questions. The goal for instruction is for it to be integrated as much as possible between the disciplines."[1] I am encouraged by schools wanting to teach this conception of humanities to young people, especially if they offer the coherence of a big theme and teach them how important it is to learn by framing questions. As someone who has championed cultural studies, I am delighted with the apparent commitment to integration between the disciplines.[2]

At this point we could pose another question: integrate what disciplines? Again, we could find a plethora of slightly different answers if we had space to consult many school districts' or college programs' descriptions. Rye Country Day School, to pluck one off the internet, speaks of the need for students to investigate the "intellectual, aesthetic, religious, philosophical, political, economic, social, and psychological" dimensions of the human experience, thereby implying a quite large array of disciplines students in their humanities track will engage.[3]

---

[1] https://sites.google.com/ramsey.k12.nj.us/k-5curriculum/grade-4/humanities#.
[2] Irene Kacandes, "German Cultural Studies: What Is at Stake?" *A User's Guide to German Cultural Studies*, eds. Scott Denham, Irene Kacandes, and Jonathan Petropoulos, University of Michigan Press, 1997, 3–28 and elsewhere.
[3] https://www.ryecountryday.org/academics/upper-school/curriculum-guide/humanities.

Whether "history" and "psychology" count as "humanities" or "social science" – these two along with "natural sciences" make up the troika of academic divisions in many North American institutions of higher education – was not really on my mind when I thought of the value of a conversation series between scholars and the general public. Rather, I was thinking much more of what seemed to be a growing gap between *my* sense of what happens on university campuses and the portrayal of it in the media and in political rhetoric. I was finding myself more and more perturbed by rampant references to the (actually ancient) metaphor of the "ivory tower" in its modern guise – that those who live the life of the mind, to use another mischievous cliché, insulate themselves from "real world problems." As if college campuses were not very much a part of the world and, as if we who worked and learned there were not actively engaging a slew of concrete challenges! At the same time, I was noticing more and more terms that were circulating outside academia without understanding of what those terms were originally coined to convey. To be sure, my discomfort reached an intolerable point when state and local governments started outlawing the teaching in public schools of "critical race theory." This specialized graduate field wasn't even taught at most colleges, much less in the elementary grades, as right-wing extremists were claiming to parents.[4]

By way of adding to the points above and creating a record of what ended up happening in "Humanities for Humans" conversations, I quote my own words from the very first session on "Racism and Fascism: A Love Story," that took place on September 27, 2022 in the home of 1014: Space for Ideas, with historian Dagmar Herzog and political scientist Michael G. Hanchard. In explaining to our audience why I coined the phrase "Humanities for Humans," I shared that:

> I wanted to bring humanities and humans together, because while I believe that humanistic study is vital to our survival, the humanities fields are under assault in this country and in other places in the world like Great Britain; whole departments are being eliminated by college administrations, and enrollments in humanities courses are declining.
>
> The humanities, as we are considering them in this series, include a large range of fields that study the arts, literature, music, philosophy, religion, and of course human endeavor of many types. Humanities scholars, to put it otherwise, have developed methods and concepts to help us better understand human behavior, organization, and creation, in the past and present. Precise verbal expression orally and in writing are hallmarks of the

---

[4] There are scores of examples. I'll admit to being gratified when a news report was made while I was writing this introduction of a school district where the population had just succeeded in removing a school board member who had banned critical race theory the very night of his installation on the board – even though this subject was not taught anywhere in the district. I heard this on my local National Public Radio station and then located a newspaper article you can find here: https://www.nytimes.com/2024/06/21/us/temecula-school-board-recall.html.

humanities fields. As teachers we strive to help our student learn how to think – not what to think – and how to then best express those thoughts to others.

In Germany and some other places, there is a strong tradition of humanities scholars as public intellectuals who are given space to share their views in venues like print journalism and radio. That's not been so much the case here in the U.S. Therefore, one goal of this series is simply to give airtime to some really smart people. To be sure, another goal is to discuss some concepts coming out of the humanities that have been accidentally or intentionally misrepresented to the general public, often as tools in the so-called culture wars. Examples include "critical race theory" and "white privilege," both originating within the academy and passing into the public sphere in ways that didn't well reflect the analytical work they were coined to do.

My observation for many years now has been not only that terms from scholars get intentionally or unintentionally misinterpreted by non-academics, but also that maybe academics spend too much time talking to each other and not enough time explaining themselves to the general public. We're calling these gatherings conversations, not just because there are two experts sitting here who will exchange ideas with each other, but also because we want this to be a conversation with you.[5]

As I look back on this project now, I suspect that my most urgent motivation was to provide a venue in which academics would not only address other "humans," of a general rather than student ilk, in clear language, providing concrete examples, but also one in which audiences could encounter academics as the pretty much normal human beings that they basically are.[6] That's why I insisted on conversations, rather than a series of lectures. I wanted audiences to observe smart people thinking on their feet in response to issues that matter to us all.[7] This desire is also behind my choice of subtitle for this volume: "Clear Thinking on Challenging Topics." To put it yet another way, I wanted the conversations and I want this book to be not just humanities *FOR* humans, but also humanities *BY* humans. I further maintain that humanities research is not of interest only within some narrow, abstract, theoretical context; individuals who study and teach these topics have a personal stake in the subjects they take up. That's another "human" in humanities.

---

5 The recordings for all sessions of "Humanities for Humans" have been put online for viewing. This quote can be found at approximately minute seven of the first session "Racism and Fascism: A Love Story." https://www.1014.nyc/humanities-for-humans.

6 I can't resist sharing an anecdote about a party I threw once when my eldest sister and brother-in-law were visiting. My well-educated brother-in-law queried me afterward: so all those folks were professors? Yes, I confirmed. They were so nice, he exclaimed with surprise.

7 The format put pressure on the contributors, since most of us are used to holding forth for fifty minutes without much interruption – pressure to respond in the moment, but also pressure to make sure to say the most important things in a very short total time.

So how did the conversation series do with these goals? Perhaps that's for others to judge and share – and I hope they still might. From my insider perspective, I would say the series has accomplished most of these goals. There were eight discussions planned to be distributed over two seasons, with two per season scheduled for interaction with a live audience invited to ask questions and two online conversations where listeners could write in questions and comments. The topics and speakers for these discussions were decided ultimately by me but in consultation with members of a board and with sponsors; sometimes I started with one speaker, and they suggested the other.[8] Of those eight planned conversations, seven took place as anticipated between two individuals with different dominant disciplinary or career foci and me as moderator. Fifteen speakers hold or held then standard academic positions at U.S. universities with one of those an active poet and another a choreographer, one is a prolific independent scholar without a formal academic appointment.[9]

Through advanced planning sessions to get to know one another and to narrow down our topic, cooperation of the speakers with series' goals and my own interruptions and questions during conversations – aimed at asking for an explanation or clarification or offering a summary I guessed audience members might be needing at that moment – I believe we succeeded in providing definitions of some important terms and in offering concrete examples, often from places and times other than our North American present, in language that was clear, intelligible and mostly free from jargon. It would have been nice to have had even more interaction with audience members. However, the restricted time formats and the large topics we assigned ourselves limited the amount of back and forth possible between experts and listeners. In the live sessions, in addition to the Q&A, a reception in a lovely space allowed audience members to speak with one another and to engage the speakers a bit further – perhaps enhancing their understandings of the topic and each other's concerns; I hope in any case making all appear more human to all. I haven't heard any reports of listeners subsequently contacting speakers whose sessions were only online. Still, interaction, particularly in the form of direct questions posed by audience members, allowed some topics to come up that we hadn't yet had a chance to discuss, often making connections to a very current hot button issue or occurrence. Though virtually all of the experts had worked to some greater or lesser extent on cultures other than

---

[8] Please see Appendix Two for list of Board members.
[9] Please consult Appendix One for the list of all speakers with exact topics and dates. See too my discussion of takeaways in the next section of this introduction. As already mentioned, you can view the actual sessions online. I'll be dedicating some space below to the May 2024 event that did not take place as originally planned.

the USA, some discussions featured more prominently than others the transatlantic and international dimensions that we also aspired to.

One regret I have is that we don't know enough about reception of the blogs, recordings, and reading lists we worked hard to create; these are all tools that the sponsors, speakers, and I hoped and still hope will lead to these topics being understood and wrestled with more deeply by an even larger number of people.[10] I originally thought that schoolteachers and professors might use the recordings or reading lists for their classes. I don't have any evidence for that yet. I also regret that the sponsors and I did not create a more formal way for audience members, whether in person or online, to provide feedback. Individuals who did contact us have been very enthusiastic about what they learned, but that could be predicted based on them taking the initiative to get in touch. It would be productive to have suggestions for improvement from those who were less satisfied. As for numbers we could track, our smallest live audience was a bit under fifty and our largest about 100.[11] The legal occupancy limit of 1014's building prevented what perhaps might have been even bigger live audiences. Online events could potentially have reached huge numbers of listeners. Given our launch after online events had already boomed and ebbed due to the pandemic lockdowns, however, that wasn't realized; still, several online "Humanities for Humans" conversations had more than one hundred individuals listening in in real time. Not to be discounted by me, anyway, are the hundreds of folks who registered for events even if they didn't end up attending or tuning in. Similar to the impressions count – the number of times someone views the internet site on which recordings are stored – these are ways in which individuals were exposed at least minimally to our topics and speakers.[12] As I told a friend once, I know there are

---

[10] From the 1014 side, some of this can be located here: https://www.1014.nyc/humanities-for-humans. Blogs sponsored by De Gruyter can be found here: https://blog.degruyter.com/tag/humanities-for-humans/. Our hope that the reading lists will prove useful is also demonstrated by their inclusion in Appendix Three of this volume.

[11] We were caught flatfooted and some of us were barricaded for a worrisome while behind police lines when then President Joe Biden made a fundraising appearance in Manhattan in May 2023, the same night as our "Reparation, Repair, Refusal" session with Marianne Hirsch and Hortense Spillers. We flipped the order of the reception and the actual event and eventually had about 100 people in the audience for the conversation itself.

[12] According to the records kept by 1014, registrations went as high as 491 for an event and impressions 2797. The number of visits and types of visitors to the blogs, impressions, or views, is particularly murky; because of German concern about privacy, the staff is not allowed to solicit information from visitors to their sites. According to Google Analytics, though, visitors for the various blogs range from 20 to 200 so far. On the positive side, there is no pressure from the publisher to take them down and due to a recent merger with Brill, there will be a new central website on which we hope the path to the blogs will be more obvious.

folks out there who must by now have seen or heard the phrase "humanities for humans" and wondered to themselves – even if only momentarily – what on earth that was supposed to mean. That reflection has a value to my sense of it, especially since those individuals might perk up when they next hear the word humanities or other terms from our individual conversation titles. I am grateful for the publication of this volume in open access as well as print, which will hopefully extend contact between our speakers and the general public.

There's no doubt that our biggest surprise with the eight events originally planned was an attempt to crash the registration website for our final May 2024 in-person discussion. A large number of registrations seemed to originate with supporters of a movement launched in January 2024 calling itself "Strike Germany" that aims to protest German government support of Israel by taking disruptive actions against German cultural organizations and events. There is no way to determine whether it was the planned topic, speakers, the series itself, or – most likely – the connection of the sponsors with Germany that made "Humanities for Humans" a target. Given recent disturbances at other German-connected cultural institutions in New York, and the protests, demonstrations, and police interventions on university campuses in the period just prior to our planned conversation, our hosts decided to cancel the event. I and the speakers were disappointed, not wanting to give in to this kind of bullying and shutting down of speech. Ultimately, though, the lack of security personnel and even adequate exits at our still unrenovated venue led to my acceptance of this decision. My fervent prayer is that the Israel-Gaza war end very soon, and, though insignificant compared to the saving of lives in that violent conflict, I hope that peace will allows us to confidently resume "Humanities for Humans" events. We were able to reschedule the important discussion with Professors Susannah Heschel and Terrence Johnson. Surely a calm examination of "Biblical Promises and Their Challenges for Religious Faith and Secular Societies Today" could contribute positively to current understandings of some aspects of world affairs.[13]

---

[13] This session took place successfully online on October 15, 2024 after the manuscript of this book had already been submitted.

Takeaways from "Humanities for Humans," 2022–2024

I hope what I have shared so far makes those of you for whom this book is a first contact with "Humanities for Humans" curious enough to want to check out the full recordings online. Precisely because those recordings are available and I hope readers of these lines will turn to them to get the full benefit of what was said on the topics of racism, fascism, inequality, reparation, repair, refusal, controversy and connection, migration, climate change, and gender, I strive to do just two things here: one is to pull out a few of the many helpful ideas that surfaced in each conversation. The other is to point out some habits of academics that were put on display during these conversations. What is below can serve in no way as "summaries," because the conversations were too rich and nuanced to summarize and also because oral speech communicates in some different ways than written speech does. Trying to capture some of that here would take up too much space in this book that has other work to do as well. For the sake of the historical record, I will take up the conversations in the order they occurred, which produces a bit of jumping back and forth in terms of some overlapping content.

"Racism and Fascism: A Love Story"

As mentioned once above, this was the inaugural session of the inaugural season. It took place on September 27, 2022, at the home of one of our sponsors 1014, that is, at 1014 Fifth Avenue in New York City. The invited experts were Michael G. Hanchard of the University of Pennsylvania, Africana Studies, Political Science departments, and Dagmar Herzog, who teaches at the City University of New York Graduate School in the fields of History, Social Welfare, Women's and Gender Studies. In choosing this topic, I was responding to the recent prominence of the term "critical race theory" in the media and on the lips of politicians; further, to the many comparisons that had been made between fascism and racism, including with the term "fascist" being applied to Donald Trump and to some of his supporters, especially to those who had participated in the January 6, 2021 insurrection at the Capitol of the United States. The idea of "a love story" came from a book that Professor Hanchard was in the process of writing, and to me it signaled the intimate connection between the two historical phenomena that would be our evening's focus.

It was a prerequisite for this session and relevant to several other conversations as well to understand that the idea of *race* has been completely discredited by genetic science despite the persistence of *racism* that is based on the false belief in race as something real that distinguishes human groups from one another. Striking formulations were produced to help bring home this fundamental point. I quoted in my introductory remarks that night author Junot Diaz's words: "Race is a monstrous fiction. Racism a monstrous crime." And Dagmar Herzog ended the evening by quoting cultural studies icon Stuart Hall's formulation that "If race is a social construct, why does racism persist? Because race is a social construct!" As Herzog then glossed it: if race were real rather than a construct, we wouldn't constantly have to justify discriminatory behavior based on it.

As for the connection between racism and fascism, I draw attention to two of the many pertinent remarks from our experts. Citing James Q. Whitman's important 2018 study, *Hitler's American Model*, and his own research on what he calls "racial rule," Michael Hanchard pointed out that the Nazis used U.S. racial laws as a kind of "play book" or in Whitman's term "model" for the Nuremburg laws, legislating ever more constrained life for those the Nazis designated Jews. Hanchard added the revealing detail that the Nazi lawyers assigned to research U.S. law were uninterested in Jim Crow laws, in contrast, because the Nazi goal was not hierarchical co-existence but rather extermination. Dagmar Herzog, who had previously made the helpful distinction between exclusionary and exterminatory racism, pointed out that the Nazis did accept co-existence with Slavs, whom they wanted – and for a time did succeed in exploiting – as slaves.

Herzog asked aloud if it was possible to have fascism without racism, citing the mixing of "races" between Italian occupiers and native Ethiopian populations and the (initially) legal acceptance of progeny born to "interracial" couples. Though ultimately both scholars produced numerous examples – including the change in attitude toward concubinage in Italian-occupied Ethiopia – that reinforced the love story between racist and fascist ideology, Herzog's example led her to a related train of thought about the importance for fascist governments of control over many aspects of sexuality. Fascists are anti-abortion, anti-gay, and believers in eugenics, she stated.

As for connections to today, Hanchard pointed to the historical facts of the major fascist regimes as all arising from within some kind of democratic polity, like the Weimar Republic in the case of Germany. Herzog backed that up with philosopher Theodor Adorno's statement that the biggest threats to democracy come from within. Many of those threats come in the form of creating alternative truths. In speaking of January 6 directly, Hanchard pointed out that the Proud Boys and the Boogaloo Boys (also Boogaloo Bois) are not aberrations, and rather, like the Ku Klux Klan, are long-lived hate groups at home in our supposed democracy.

One final aspect of this conversation I have space to include is that both scholars shared recent research and its significance in revising the narratives we tell ourselves, like the one just mentioned about needing to include the presence of hate groups in the story we tell about U.S. democracy. A further example was offered by Herzog: with the Fall of the Berlin Wall and its concomitant opening up of archives in the former East Germany, analysis of newly available documents reveals that Nazi euthanasia programs were not as ideologically consistent as they had previously been thought to be by historians. The mentally disabled who were the main targets of the T-4 extermination program were actually sorted by whether or not they could contribute labor. Those who could work were not killed. Those who could not, were. Such correction of our understanding of the past or present as new evidence surfaces is of course fundamental to scholarly projects.

Many characteristics of scholar-teachers as I know them surfaced in this conversation as in others. Hanchard and Herzog listened carefully to each other and were polite even when they disagreed on finer points. This respect extended to the audience to whom they listened attentively and asked clarification of when some questions were not clear or succinct. The atmosphere created, I point out, was quite different from the adversarial ones of many talk radio or TV talk shows.

"Imagining Anew the Future of the Earth"

What I aspired to for our second session, the first online conversation, was to air what might be missing when we hear mostly about the quantifiable sides of climate change from scientists – which of course is also important to continue to do. I found my way to two individuals I had never met before with the help of some of my Dartmouth colleagues. The conversation took place on December 8, 2022 between myself; Harriet Hawkins, a trained geographer specializing in the field of GeoHumanities, often collaborating with practicing artists and employed at Royal Holloway, University of London; and Rebecca Tsosie, a trained lawyer and philosopher, who in addition to those subjects teaches Indigenous Studies at the University of Arizona.

A somewhat inverse parallel prerequisite to that in the previous conversation with regard to the established scientific discrediting of the idea of different human races, could be the scientific agreement beyond a doubt that human consumption of fossil fuels has caused an increase in atmospheric temperatures and changes to some features of the earth. Rebecca Tsosie reminded us that global consensus has already been established and ratified through the United Nations with the help of Western science: change is real, and some has already taken place.

In addition to reference to international actions, two reframings came out of this conversation that I consider particularly productive for thinking about future action: drawing on the human capacity for imagination and drawing on the profoundly different ways of thinking by Indigenous communities about the human relationship to the earth and natural resources.

Consideration of exact language and its effects is fundamental to humanities, and it was on frequent display in this conversation. Both Hawkins and Tsosie stated explicitly that language matters. When we use the phrase "climate change," it is as if no one is responsible; it has just somehow happened. We need to put the *human* back into the naming of the problem or at least into the discussion of it. Both speakers also agreed that unfortunately, there's no perfect phrase to signal what is going on. Hawkins has gravitated toward the phrase "earth futures," though that too doesn't reference human agency strongly enough. The idea of imagining (different) futures is implied in it, though, and the need for imagination came up repeatedly in the conversation (and in almost all the other conversations). Another example of the power of words came through the concept of "degrowth"; to pronounce the word is to point in a direction that many people may never have considered before. What future could we imagine our way to if we were going in the opposite direction of "growth, growth, growth"?[14] Another way in which imagination came up was through Hawkins's observation that the changes we have caused to the environment themselves represent a previous failure of Western imagination to consider where growth mentality would take us.

Tsosie pointed out that the word "crisis" can be paralyzing instead of aiding people to action. She also reminded us that the American environmental ethos is "utilitarian": water, air, and other natural treasures are thought of as resources to be used, and the use of resources is granted to someone or some entity. It hasn't mattered if that grantee wastes them. Our current Western legal framework cannot stop the kinds of activities we're engaged in that are damaging the environment. Tsosie welcomes recent international treaties and declarations that are beginning to acknowledge Indigenous peoples' rights, particularly because Indigenous ways of knowing are "place-based" and "multigenerational." Tsosie also used the word "attunement," speaking of the way Indigenous peoples are attuned to their environments, an attunement that allows them to register changes and respond to those changes. Building Indigenous caretaking of place into our legal and ideological frameworks would allow us to imagine things like a river having rights, and indeed Tsosie has been involved in discussions about the competition of rights-holders to water in the Colorado River: will there be any water left? Does the Colorado River itself have a right to continue to exist? Tsosie cited the inspiring example of the Maori winning rights analogous to human rights for the Whanganui River, which itself now has legal standing and guardians to speak for it in legal contexts.[15]

---

14 https://degrowth.info/en/degrowth.
15 https://www.theguardian.com/world/2017/mar/16/new-zealand-river-granted-same-legal-rights-as-human-being.

In responding to my query about the role art can play in our future interactions with the environment, Hawkins reminded us that artists are themselves great imaginers. She reported on several projects where the creating of something or the "doing of it," led to visualizing environmental change in ways that just reading the facts of it might not. She had as a visual background for our zoom an ice cave that she appeared to be sitting in, and she pointed out the location of a set of stairs leading to the ice cave that was actually quite far from where the ice began. To walk those stairs and then to the entrance demonstrated how far that particular glacier had shrunk since the stairs had been constructed. In a physical sense, one could walk the shrinking of the glacier, thereby taking in the reality of that environmental change through one's body.

"Systemic Inequalities: Is Change Possible?"

The third conversation in the series also took place online on March 9, 2023 when I spoke with historian Robin D. G. Kelley, of the University of California at Los Angeles, and Bruce Robbins, of Columbia University, teaching in a program called Humanities, and also in the department of English and Comparative Literature. Kelley and Robbins had been institutional colleagues for a number of years at Columbia, and they were familiar with each other's work. My initial goals were to probe what I considered an explosion in distribution of wealth and hence of growing inequalities, as well as get to some relevant terms I considered misunderstood in the public sphere, particularly the terms "systemic" and "intersectionality." We did get to these goals in a sense, but a (polite and indirect) rejection of my opening statements by Professor Kelley allowed a different framework to emerge first.

Inequality is itself a relative measure, Kelley began; it's a chimera – as if there were only a finite amount of wealth out there. We need to ask where the wealth comes from, he continued, how it is generated – and that's by forcing communities and nations into debt. Ultimately, the problem is capitalism and exploitation of labor. We can ask how we got here, and he would call that not an explosion, but a series of explosions, some of which Kelley then helpfully reviewed.

Robbins's book *The Beneficiary*, also became a structuring element to probe inequalities. As Robbins summarized it for the "Humanities for Humans" audience that day, his intention in that book was not to make all Westerners or today's wealthy "feel guilty," but rather to change the terms in which they think about poverty and inequality. Paraphrasing himself, Robbins explained that instead of thinking of poverty in humanitarian terms – oh, it's scandalous; as a human I should do something – he wants people to realize that there's a causal relationship between me having this and them not. *We* did the underdeveloping of the so-called underdeveloped world. That brought the discussion back to the importance of knowing history.

The power of language came up in this conversation several times; to cite one, Robbins talked about the effectiveness of slogans, quoting and glossing the phrase: No Manchester without Mississippi! Kelley made clear his dislike of the phrase "white privilege" which I had brought up, because he believes it makes white workers think they have things they actually do not and prevents them from seeing their commonalities with other workers.

As much as both participants joked about hoping the revolution "happens on Tuesday," Robbins wanted to emphasize that there are some things we can do within the system we have. He pointed to reform of finance laws; it wasn't just a few bad apples; it was the system that was allowing all to do what they were doing legally; the laws had to be changed to prevent that. He suggested that if we want to fight inequality, we should get together with like-minded people and change other laws. Medicare for All would help with the wildly unequal access to healthcare in the U.S.A., for instance. So, we could decide to work for that. Agreeing, Kelley brought to bear several historical moments including in the wake of the Second World War with the founding of the United Nations and in the 1960s with the proposals of the G-77. To my query about solutions, Kelley observed: There has been no shortage of solutions. The problem is not good solutions to make the world a more equitable place, but rather that such solutions have been beaten down by those who have a stake in maintaining the status quo.

Several moments during the conversation involved reference to disciplinary practices, as when Robbins put forward that though he doesn't consider himself good at "the practical," he is good at "slow change," at helping his students develop "common sense." In one of the most positive statements of the conversation, he declared himself convinced that "common sense can change even more." In that vein, though claiming that literature professors are not good at concrete examples, he offered one himself: in our current moment, changes in the common sense around the plague of mass incarceration seem to be adding up to a consensus for prison reform. Kelley expressed the need for more common sense with regard to the category of class and the need to understand it with reference to other exploitations. To this end he quoted Stuart Hall's definition of race as "a modality through which class is lived for people who are racialized." This is one formulation that reveals the concept of intersectionality. Kelley spelled it out by saying that class oppression feeds off racism, gender oppressions, sexuality oppression, and more; it can never make sense – it simply isn't possible – to limit ourselves to a discussion of "just" class.

As in several other conversations, the imagination was cited as necessary for change. Kelley urged us to imagine what it means to live in a society "where it's anathema for anyone not to have a place to live; where social housing is not a concept, it's just simply part of life. Imagine what that means!" And we ended the conversation with a paraphrasing of the conclusion of Robbins's *Beneficiary*: you cannot change things unless you can sense that they can be otherwise.

"Repair, Reparation, Refusal"

The first season concluded with another in-person conversation at 1014 Fifth Avenue. Marianne Hirsch, of Columbia University, Comparative Literature, Women's and Gender Studies spoke with Hortense Spillers, of Vanderbilt University, English. Hirsch and Spillers have known each other for many years and at the time of our meeting had both recently retired from their institutions. For the record, I have had the privilege of knowing Hirsch and Spillers since early in my career, and they were the first pair who agreed to a "Humanities for Humans" conversation, though it had to be scheduled for the end of the first season.

My original motivation for this session was to clarify some terms that I believed many members of the general public did not understand well, the three R's of our title. There had been renewed discussion of reparations and controversy around it in some local contexts and mostly just politicized hot air at the national level.[16] Repair and refusal are obviously common words, but ones which have been used to point at certain efforts and attitudes among academics in light of ongoing racism and discrimination. A bit differently to the other sessions, we included concrete definitional work on the reading list itself, not just through the book titles that take up those subjects, but also by grouping the entries and defining words there.

Hortense Spillers launched the conversation itself in the eloquent language that is her hallmark:

> I cannot think of a more timely and urgent subject than repair, reparation, and refusal since it seems to me that these three concepts touch the pulse of our collective anxiety right now: repair to our broken covenants that make possible a democratic republic supposedly predicated on the rule of law, reparation to communities long denied the full blessings of

---

[16] See for instance the controversy over Bruce's Beach in California.
https://www.nrdc.org/stories/once-thriving-black-owned-beach-returned-its-rightful-owners#:~:text=The%20victory%20at%20California's%20Bruce's,land%20restitution%20for%20Black%20Americans.&text=Like%20millions%20of%20others%20before,to%20California%20with%20a%20dream.

the rule of law, and refusal to surrender to the totalitarian dangers and impulses that threaten to engulf us.

After quoting part of Lincoln's first inaugural address, Spillers turned more explicitly to our country's relationship to "Africanity or Blackness" and specifically to the "severe protocol of discipline and punishment, of surveillance and containment that is nothing short of terrorism as political practice" – a terrorism against Black males that is not new and yet seems to possess a new lethal energy in the post-Obama era. Naming recent victims and their mothers, Spillers asked if "these mothers of dead sons can ever be compensated for their loss," and, if not, how we can translate human hurt into law. What ultimately might be the differences between repair and reparation?

Though I believe Spillers was not intending any personal rebuke, I accepted and accept her powerful words as judgement of my naivete around the benefit of stating facts and offering definitions. Reflective silence seemed the only possible if inadequate response to the invocation of this violence, as much as the pain of it and my agenda of "having a conversation on a difficult topic" made me want to rush forward. Marianne Hirsch urged us: "We have to sit with these names, these stories. We have to take in this pain." Hirsch's next gesture involved sharing what she has learned from Spillers's work: "You have spoken about the irreparability of the high crimes against the flesh. You have enjoined us to change our language, our ways of thinking. We need to transform the grammar of our speaking to recognize and acknowledge family, kinship, the body. The way I read your work is as a work of refusal: refusal to accept the status quo, refusal to accept the way we've been using language."

Spillers accepted Hirsch's characterization of "refusal" and then suggested that a start in the direction of the road that might lead to repair would be acknowledging that something has happened, acknowledging that people were not making things up, acknowledging that that something that has happened is *enormous*. An example that came up a bit later in this conversation concerned the process carried out by the Truth and Reconciliation Committee (TRC); in the wake of the dismantling of apartheid in South Africa, the TRC made some contribution toward moving forward as a nation if not to healing through honest public acknowledgment of terrible crimes.

Hirsch shared some with us about why repair has become so important to her and the set of activities that she and others have been involved in that they've named the "Zip Code Memory Project." A major first step in that context has been to acknowledge that the losses of the Covid-19 pandemic were very differently distributed in participants' neighborhoods. This entailed acknowledging too that something is broken, that the system was and is working badly, and that the damage can't necessarily be repaired but that something could perhaps be built on already existing networks of mutual aid. I won't say more here, since Hirsch gives a more detailed explanation of this project in her contribution to this book than time permitted that evening.

Some academic reflexes that I think this conversation demonstrated include the precise and indeed eloquent language of both speakers that I have already quoted, as well as the framing of questions to show precisely that sometimes even germane and well-worded questions cannot be answered adequately with words or logic. There was also respectful disagreement with me at one point for suggesting that maybe we needed to "recognize resilience," with Spillers pondering whether the development of modes of survival in Black communities could have something to do with what I was calling resilience, and Hirsch objecting to the concept because it puts pressure and responsibility on the people who are suffering. It's not that the mothers Spillers named and other groups of mothers Hirsch went on to name are not resilient, but rather than we should be supporting them with calls for justice. And in reminding us of the Argentinian mothers and grandmothers of the Disappeared protesting at the Plaza de Mayo, Hirsch glossed their demand – We want them back alive! – as a refusal, a refusal of the gesture that erases the memory that these people ever even existed. To demand them back alive is to articulate that "we cannot accept (any of) these deaths and yet we live with them." This brought us to the power of art, as in the climate change discussion: art as creating, as communicating something with which those of us who are not direct targets nor directly bereaved otherwise would have no real contact, no real connection to without exposure to the art work.

Importantly, to my mind, our two speakers ended, however, not with the power of art or memorialization, but with the necessity of protest. Spillers remarked that, "Nothing is going to save us outside of ourselves. Thoughts and prayers are not enough. I'm 80 years old, and I'm going to have to be out there, arthritis or not." Hirsch agreed: "We have to get out in the street! We have to stay out there. We have to fight parasitical whiteness, too."

"Gender, Desire, Embodiment"

The conversation series opened its second season on October 18, 2023 with the important topic of gender. The goal here was not so much to review the dreadful inauguration of laws trying to dictate who uses what bathroom or, much more consequential, who is allowed to get gender-affirming medical care and who not, but rather to talk about gender as a path to desire. Meg Fernandes, Poet and Adjunct Professor and Writer-in-Residence at Lafayette College, spoke with Jack Halberstam of Columbia University, Professor of Gender Studies and English. The two are friends and referred frequently to previous discussions they had had concerning Fernandes's poems or films and events they'd recently attended. One of Fernandes's poems is even called, "Dinner with Jack."[17]

I launched us with a short recital of how differently the word "gender" itself has been deployed over the course of my lifetime: from grammatical gender to a code word for "women" to its expansion to something constituent of all human bodies to something that we perform. I ended that list by quoting a memorable recent definition of gender by Masha Gessen that seemed to me to incorporate the spirit of the particular kind of conversation we were hoping would unfold that evening: "Gender is something that happens between me and other people."[18]

Such a definition would not have been possible without two pathbreaking books of Judith Butler, *Gender Trouble: Feminism and the Subversion of Identity* (1990) and *Bodies That Matter: On the Discursive Limits of Sex* (1993). Halberstam explained that through these studies, Butler moved attention away from queer and trans people to straight people. In Halberstam's summary "gender isn't simply a pathology when we see how it's acted out through queer bodies; gender is a problem for all bodies. All bodies, Butler said, are performing their gender." We entered the twenty-first century, Halberstam proposed, "fully aware that gender was a construction, but that it feels real, that it is the basis for all kinds of oppression and all kinds of pleasure, and that gender and sexual politics must not circle around identitarian claims." As for the concept of the non-binary, Halberstam narrated that he had to be "schooled in it" by younger people. For him, gender was a conduit to desire. But he came to understand that for a large swath of people, non-binary became a way to reject an entire gender system. When someone says they're non-binary, Halberstam suggested, "they're saying yes, something about the surface of the body, and they're also saying something much bigger than that. They're saying no to this shitty world that older generations are passing on to them."

Meg Fernandes began by talking about desire as a triangulating structure. "You can't want what you already have. It's always you, what you want, and that sort of obstacle in between. This is why boundlessness, orifices, and interiority, these openings, and borderless, somewhat unknowable phenomena, are interest-

---

[17] Meg Fernandes, "Dinner with Jack," *I Do Everything I'm Told*, Tin House, 2023, 5.
[18] "We Need Better Narratives About Gender," a conversation between Masha Gessen and Lydia Polgreen on the Ezra Klein Show, October 10, 2023. What it means to understand queer life more expansively. https://www.nytimes.com/2023/10/10/opinion/ezra-klein-podcast-masha-gessen-oct-2023.html.

ing to me." Fernandes posited an intimate relationship between language and queer bodies by adding that "one way in which bodies have knowledges that are queer are these kinds of interior private knowledges that you develop when you have to learn about another person's body or your own body that is nowhere in the culture: 'this is what you call this part of my body.' Everything becomes discursive. And at that moment, when you put into language what this thing is supposed to mean to this one person that is not reproducible in any other person, you realize it reflects back something about heterosexual culture."

The topic of current fear and obsession in the public sphere about queer, trans-, and non-binary bodies was also discussed, even as it was not our focus. Halberstam suggested that this fear has a very intimate source because a larger percentage than we might suspect of the younger generation does not identify as normative gender or heterosexual in any uncomplicated way.[19] Conservatives are worried, not because the threat to gender stability is "out there," but because it's in their own homes.

In addition to Meg Fernandes's poems themselves, several cultural productions were recommended and discussed, including the novel *Manhunt* by Gretchen Felker-Martin (2022); the book *Testo-Junkie* by Paul Preciado, subtitled "Sex, Drugs and Biopolitics in the Pharmacopornographic Era" (originally published in Spanish and French in 2008, and in English translation in 2013); the film *Orlando: My Political Biography* by Preciado (2023, and based on Virginia Woolf's 1928 novel *Orlando*); the artwork of Kent Monkman; as well as the 1970s "anarchitecture" of artist Gordon Matta-Clark.

The final note of the evening was sounded by Meg Fernandes, reciting some favorite lines from the essay "Lovers and Fighters" (pub. 2006) by lawyer and trans-activist Dean Spade:

> One of my goals in thinking about redefining the way we view relationships is to try to treat the people I date more like I treat my friends – to be respectful and thoughtful and have boundaries and reasonable expectations – and to try to treat my friends more like my dates – to give them special attention, honor my commitments to them, be consistent, and invest deeply in our futures together.

Fernandes commented: "For years I had that above my bed. It's changed my life. I love my life because of that commitment. So that's something I would end on."

And that is, in fact, what we did: end that conversation with this positive and constructive commitment.

---

19 For one recent survey that includes countries beside the U.S., see https://www.ipsos.com/en/ipsos-pride-survey-2024-gen-zers-most-likely-identify-lgbt.

"World on the Move"

"World on the Move" was the title agreed to by migration experts Kathryn Abrams of the University of California at Berkeley, a legal scholar and professor, and Mark Terkessidis, an independent scholar based in Berlin, Germany. The conversation took place online on December 7, 2023. Abrams and Terkessidis had never met prior to our online planning session. I have known Abrams for decades and had collaborated with her before, whereas I had only read Terkessidis's work before making his acquaintance and asking him to participate.

This conversation afforded additional examples not just of respectful disagreement but where such disagreement produced enormously productive reframings of the topic under examination. Though I began the session by stating the generally accepted current number of people displaced from their homes – about 110 million according to the United Nations – I also immediately added that numbers would not be our concern today. Terkessidis politely began his remarks by saying that, actually, he would like to talk about numbers. He proceeded to make two very helpful observations about this "110 million" that gets trotted out so frequently in conjunction with the topic of migration, whether in Europe where he lives, or in the United States or elsewhere. We might have a "record number of people on the move," he agreed, "but we also have a record number of people on earth!" When this 110 million is evoked to frighten people, he admonished us, we also need to realize that all 110 million are *not* amassed at the borders of Europe nor at the southern border of the United States. Rather, most refugees have fled either to other locations within their home countries or to neighboring countries.

While my own previous research into refugeedom had confirmed Terkessidis's second point, I realized at the moment he made his remarks that I had no idea what the total world population was at the time of what I and others have cited as the previous high mark of people on the move, the end of the Second World War; I did know that estimates of refugees in those years are as varied as 40–60 million. Nor did I have a very precise idea of the current world population that could provide a truer comparison of today's numbers to those of the mid-twentieth century. Despite not having available for calculation the exact numbers needed, I immediately suspected that today's numbers might produce a smaller percentage than then. Spontaneously and enthusiastically, I not only conceded Terkessidis's points, I admitted my ignorance and thanked him profusely for having offered these correctives.[20]

---

20 I have looked up the numbers in the interim, and Terkessides's point was and is extremely well-taken; depending on exactly which statistical sources one puts into the calculation, the per-

Kathryn Abrams provided a different but similarly helpful reframing of the migration issue. When I'd precirculated possible questions we could discuss, I was thinking very much within the framework of "receiving nations," and what individuals in those nations could do to help migrants and work for better immigration laws. Abrams began with quite a different question: what puts us into the position of making decisions about where other people live? There's a complicated historical and legal answer for that, of course, some of which Abrams succinctly provided with regard to assumptions about the sovereignty of nation-states to control their borders. But what if we considered, as Abrams did borrowing from Ayelet Shachar, that there exists a "birthright lottery," and we just happened to have won it?[21] Abrams found attractive but ultimately too unlikely for adoption Shachar's novel idea to tax intergenerational transmission of citizenship similar to the way some countries tax inheritance; the proceeds could fund infrastructure in those countries from which people are fleeing because they can't feed themselves and their families there. Abrams would amend this by suggesting that we should be willing to face challenges, diminished profits, and changes to our way of life; a similar point was made by Robbins in the Inequality discussion.

Instead of the "blood or soil" framework which Shachar's ideas are still within, we could opt, Abrams proposed, to create radically new bases for recognizing membership in a nation. What if we considered the extent to which an individual participates in reciprocal exchange with the society they would like to become a part of? Abrams gave some examples of contributions migrants make to their would-be new homes.[22] Terkessidis was speaking to the same larger point when he reminded us that the kind of welfare states that exist in Europe cannot open borders completely without collapsing, and that we urgently need discussion about what should constitute membership in the democratic welfare state. Such discussion is absent from public discourse about current policies.

As in other "Humanities for Humans" conversations, words and the work they do, as well as frameworks and narratives, came up frequently. Both experts agreed that "migration as a problem," is a narrative of threat that needs to be transformed. Abrams pointed out that our narratives always seem to begin at the U.S. / Mexico border and leave out the history of American interventions that cre-

---

centage of refugees to world population today is somewhere around 1.37%; whereas, again, depending on the exact sources of your numbers for the mid-twentieth century, the percentage of refugees to world population was something like 2.17%. I used figures from "Worldometer."

21 Ayelet Shachar, *The Birthright Lottery: Citizenship and Global Inequality*, Harvard University Press, 2009.

22 Readers of this introduction can find more details, of course, in the recording of the whole conversation, and also in the contribution that Abrams makes to this volume.

ated the disastrous status quo in many Latin American countries from which people flee; the effects of NAFTA on Mexico are also absent from our migration narrative. As for the phrase "border crisis," for most politicians and those listening to them, it simply refers to the number of people at the border, whereas that phrase should also apply to the unwillingness of governments to provide a response, as well as to the humanitarian disasters that those failures have caused.

As for what we citizens can do, our experts suggested intervening at the local level; we can start by taking time to decide what we think we owe to those who are on the move. Terkessidis and Abrams pointed to the act of "accompaniment" of migrants, quite a lot of which took place in Germany in the first years after the arrival there of more than a million Syrian refugees and more recently with the influx of refugees from the Russian invasion of Ukraine. Abrams mentioned a group of law students and others she works with in the U.S. who do concrete things to help migrants make bail when they have been detained. I cited examples I knew from Germany as well as the American Midwest where residents helped new arrivals learn the local language.

I haven't mentioned often enough in these short accounts that excellent comments and concrete suggestions also flowed in from the audience. On the occasion of this conversation, listeners used the chat function to share short testimonials of aid given that they knew of, like translating for migrants during interviews or legal hearings.

"Controversy as a Tool for Connection"

My penultimate assignment in this section is to share a few words about the conversation between Liz Lerman, choreographer, teacher, writer, and Martha Minow of Harvard University, legal scholar and professor, which took place online on February 21, 2024. As with a few of our other pairs, Lerman and Minow knew each other and had even collaborated in the creation of "Small Dances About Big Ideas," a performance commissioned by the Harvard Law School to commemorate the sixtieth anniversary of the start of the Nuremberg Trials. I had been inspired for years by Minow's work and was delighted when she agreed to speak in the series and suggested Liz Lerman as a conversation partner. While I, alas, had not been familiar with Lerman's large and varied body of work, I had hoped from the start of the project that something related to dance could be included, because for me dance is such an important language of the humanistic spirit and study of dance such a dynamic part of academic humanities. So, I was particularly pleased when Minow suggested Lerman, and the two of them decided that they wanted to focus on how we can turn controversy into connection. The inability to have substantive discussion among people who disagree has struck me as more and more the modus vivendi of the United States, and it was a motivating factor for me in conceiving of the "Humanities for Humans" conversation series.

I needn't say too much more here, because a large section of this conversation is reproduced later in this book. I was pleased that Lerman and Minow agreed to its inclusion because in this fashion readers of this volume can get a better sense of the style of these conversations, at least when put into written form, which is different both from the oral instantiation and how it would read if it had been written to be read rather than being a lightly edited transcript of an oral interaction.[23]

One thing I didn't expect was that Minow would take up the title of the series in such a meaningful way, so I would like to highlight that here: "I'm thinking right now about the words that make up the name of this conversation series: 'Humanities for Humans,'" she said. "They make me reflect that I am drawn constantly to that basic question. If we're dealing with humans, isn't that something that we have in common, that we are human? Can't being human be a starting point for connection?" This in turn triggered recital of a scene known to Minow from her work on the genocide in Rwanda in which one individual was precisely *not* proceeding from the starting point that the children around him were human, referring to them rather as "vermin."

Framing and frameworks is a topic within this discussion. There is a moment when Lerman points to what she has just said as a reframing. She's responding to a question typed into the chat by a listener in Tel Aviv who's concerned that we are only telling one side of the narrative of the violence being perpetrated in Israel-Gaza. Lerman refers back to something she had already explained earlier in the conversation – a set of "miracles" that she had composed when she was struggling particularly hard with the Israel-Gaza war during Hannukah 2023. I quote Lerman:

> I feel for the person who wrote in that question. I don't know that this is adequate, but I mentioned earlier, the eight days of Miracles that I wrote during Hanukkah. It may not

---

[23] Having worked with transcripts for several of my earlier articles and books, I can attest that most people are surprised at how incoherent even highly eloquent people appear to be when their speech is faithfully transcribed. Most speakers utilize "you know," "ummm," "like" much more than they or their listeners realize. Such fillers were mainly removed as you'll see below. You can find some of my own wrestling with the difference between oral and written communication in my book, *Talk Fiction: Literature and the Talk Explosion*, University of Nebraska Press, 2001; and in the previously mentioned *Daddy's War: Greek American Stories. A Paramemoir*, University of Nebraska Press, 2009.

meet the desires of the listener, but on day three, I wrote of the miraculous return of those raped to death. In my miracle, their pelvises are now intact; their heads are back on their bodies, which bear no bruises from having been dragged through the streets; the bodies torn apart by bomb after bomb are back in place where they were put by God, by Allah, by Buddha or by the Divine Sacred.

In this example, you see me again framing bigger and yet still trying to include the specifics and the horrors of what happened. (italics added by IK)

The last sentence is what academics sometimes refer to as "meta-analysis," jumping to a different level for the purpose of labeling and identifying the operation of analysis. The value of achieving a larger framing had already been discussed by Lerman and Minow, and at this moment Lerman is pointing out the way she did that both by referring to different acts of desecrating bodies that had happened in different locations and also by using four different names for the creator of those bodies: God, Allah, Buddha, the Divine Sacred. I found myself particularly delighted that this gesture is so clearly performed by someone whose main occupation is not within the academy, or maybe I should specify, who is not trained in literary theory, since those of us with that kind of training seem to refer most frequently to the "meta-level."[24] I hasten to remind that Lerman is a professor; she has a teaching position at Arizona State University, and she mentions several times during the conversation some of her teaching techniques and how much she learns from her students.

A final special moment for me, anyway, is another example of experts not necessarily rejecting my own framing, but certainly reframing or shifting it. In this case, I asked whether or not we needed to consider "love" in our discussion. Minow immediately calls that a "tall order" for the contexts we've been discussing – echoing for me Hirsch's discomfort with my query about "resilience" – and she pivots, as did Hirsch, to something she thinks is more helpful: in this case, to the idea of a mediator; that sometimes you can't fix controversy alone. Lerman reflects aloud on the word "love," and offers a different context, a different meaning – a meaning and context that maybe we don't always think of when we use the word love, she suggests.

Which brings me to a final comment about these "misunderstanding" or "disagreements." Sometimes it is as helpful to academic work – really, I wager, to progress in thinking of any kind – to figure out what does not fit as to figure out what does. I am reminded of a beloved professor of poetry recently deceased, Helen Vendler, who suggested to us teaching fellows during my graduate school

---

[24] The 2021 rebranding of Facebook to "Meta" is another frustrating example, to my mind, of a useful term from academia being circulated in the public sphere in a misleading way that obscures the intellectual work of the concept.

years, that in asking why the poet used this exact word, you can ask what other words could have been there and yet are not – why they don't suit as well. What different meaning or direction would that other word have taken us to? Why is this the one the poet ultimately chose?

This seems like a good note with which to conclude my mention of this conversation, because I consider highly productive these moments where our specialists disagreed with a word, a phrase or a question I asked. I don't remember ever taking it as a put-down. We actually "connected" intellectually at these moments, examining together, in a sense, why this word or phrase works better for this situation under discussion. Perhaps I am spelling this out here because, again, my sense of our current moment is one in which somehow insulting one's interlocutor seems to be admired rather than condemned. As Lerman and Minow's conversation makes clear, that certainly does not lead to connection.

A conversation we had tentatively titled **"Organized Religion, Religious Hate, and the Future of Secular Societies"** was to have taken place in person in the building at 1014 Fifth Avenue on May 6, 2024, between Susannah Heschel, my colleague at Dartmouth College, member of the Religion Department and frequent chair of the Jewish Studies Program, and Terrence Johnson, a professor at the Harvard Divinity School, specializing in African American religious studies. The upcoming talk had been advertised with the following short blurb:

> Many heinous actions reported in recent news are linked to individuals or groups that claim to be people of faith. Our two experts in religious studies will consider some consequences of engaging with Judeo-Christian scripture and its relevancy for the current, alas violent, political moment.

The crashing of the registration site already recounted earlier in this introduction that caused this event to be postponed occurred just days before Professors Heschel, Johnson and I were scheduled to meet to specify the topic further and, so, that discussion never took place. As of the time of this writing, the public conversation has not yet been rescheduled, though that is still my strong hope and that of the sponsors.[25]

The very last words I would like to utter in this section, concern, I hope, pointing out the obvious. I learned so much myself through these conversations and they could not have happened without the contribution of many individuals. I am enormously grateful to all the scholars who agreed to participate and who

---

[25] As noted in an earlier footnote, we were able to hold this important discussion online on October 15, 2024. The new title and focus were: "Biblical Promises and Their Challenges for Religious Faith and Secular Societies." It was too late, however, to add a summary to this volume.

shared things they know so generously and cogently. And I offer also a huge thanks to the staff members of 1014 and to staff and editors at De Gruyter who contributed in numerous ways that allowed these conversations to take place.

What to expect in this book

The short essays that follow are all penned by individuals who spoke in a conversation of the "Humanities for Humans" series. However, not all individuals who spoke in that series were able to contribute here. Those who do, write about topics related to the topics they conversed about. But this is not a repetition. As I've mentioned a few times, the recordings of actual sessions and the blogs from a handful of them will continue to have an online life. What follows here then is an enhancement to those original conversations, a new opportunity to hear from some very smart people and to learn more of what they know. My hope is that these essays also serve as an opportunity to get to know better some academics by learning more about them personally, and also by observing how they think – on this occasion not so much by listening to them respond, as by noticing how they decide to express themselves in writing, written communication being different than oral, something I have pointed out a few times above.

To this second goal, then, I have asked scholars to introduce themselves by speaking in their own first person. And I have grouped the essays by the mode that I believe dominates in their particular essay: naming a problem, probing its stakes, or crafting connections to other issues and solutions. In my estimation, each of these essays does each of these things, but in some, one activity stands out the most.

In Part One, Naming the Problem, the first essay by Dagmar Herzog offers us clear definitions of key terms like racism and fascism. Herzog also makes connections between racism and fascism and shows how aspects of those ideologies led to further phenomena like eugenics and euthanasia. In the second essay I've placed in this section, Michael G. Hanchard spells out his concept of "racial regimes," and he demonstrates what is at stake in not recognizing the racial rule in nominally democratic polities, thereby allowing fascist and authoritarian tendencies to develop. And in the third essay, Kathryn Abrams names flawed assumptions in thinking about migrants and the qualities they bring to their new polities, those misapprehensions leading not only to further discrimination against migrants but also to our own impoverishment as a society.

To be sure, naming and defining are also present in the three essays in Part Two. Still, I've placed three contributions together to highlight the urgency the writers express over what is at stake having named and analyzed a problem.

Bruce Robbins examines "equality" and its changing position in academic discussions over the last fifty years or so in a journey toward revealing what is at stake in moral equivalencies being articulated at the beginning of the Israeli-Gaza conflict, the time at which he composed this essay. Robin D. G. Kelley, writing some seven months after the beginning of that war, works his way from what is at stake in academic settings like the one he participated in with "Humanities for Humans" to what is at stake when universities are acting like fascist regimes in reaction to student protest to what is at stake when we are witnessing genocide. Readers will encounter similar urgency over our responsibilities in Rebecca Tsosie's consideration of whether we can learn from Indigenous practices of sustainability and ethics of place to protect the earth we all depend on. The writers in Part Three are no less urgent nor are they dealing with lesser problems, but the emphases in the three contributions I've grouped in this part relate to solutions, and particularly how we can craft connections to one another and to the problems that urgently need solving. Harriet Hawkins waters some seeds she began to sow in the original "Humanities for Humans" conversation with regard to the power of the imagination to lead us toward a liveable future. Liz Lerman and Martha Minow share a number of strategies they have deployed for quite different contexts from one-on-one personal discussions to feedback on artistic projects to reconciliation in post-genocidal communities. As mentioned earlier, their contribution here is a lightly edited version of parts of the transcript of the actual conversation that took place in February 2024. Marianne Hirsch provides more details on the project she had described briefly in her discussion with Hortense Spillers of the Zip Code Memory Project to the end of illustrating how academic discussions of trauma and postmemory can transform to consideration of historical accountability, justice, and reparation.

Part One: **Naming the Problem**

Dagmar Herzog
Racism, Fascism, Eugenics: The Political Work of Consequential Fictions

Dagmar Herzog and I have known each other for several decades. We became acquainted through three very special academic contexts: an unusual annual gathering referred to as "The Northeast Workshop on German Women's History and Literature," that brought women academics in history together with women academics in literature/cultural studies to discuss over two days a particular theme, sometimes a specific book, related to Germany; a biannual conference on "Lessons and Legacies of the Holocaust," also an interdisciplinary group; and at the annual conferences of the German Studies Association, the largest professional association bringing together academics in many disciplines to discuss a wide range of topics related to Germany and other German-speaking countries, regions, groups, or individuals, which I also mentioned earlier in this book. I got to observe Herzog not only as an extremely well-read and articulate person, but also as someone who is deeply insightful in responding to other people's work. Not all academics are good at this, and Herzog and some of the other German women historians I got to know in these settings really inspired me to try to be smart, respectful, and constructive when giving feedback.

This is what Dagmar Herzog shares with us about her life's journey so far:

No one who knew me as a teenager or early twenty-something could have guessed that I would become a historian. In fact, when I began attending college at Duke University in the late 1970s, I thought the field was so far away from the things I hoped to learn that I initially pleaded with the school's administrators – successfully – that I be allowed to count a religion course as sufficient for fulfilling every student's requirement to take a history class. By my senior year, I realized how wrong I had been and took – and loved – two history courses, one on civil rights and the other on comparative slave societies. Still, I didn't think there would be more history in my future. My double major at Duke was in French Literature and Political Science. And I had completed half of my Political Science credits by taking courses on criminal justice at the American University in Washington, D.C., while pursuing a practicum as an Investigator for the Public Defender Service – a job that might best be described as detective work on behalf of underresourced, systemically disempowered clients.

Raised in the U.S. South by German immigrant parents who were deeply involved in the African American civil rights movement through churches and antipoverty programs, I also spent recurrent stretches of my childhood and adolescence back among extended family in Germany, including a summer working in a legendary German charity institution for people with varieties of cognitive impairment at which two of my great-aunts were employed. Care work made sense to me, and after graduation from Duke, I returned to Washington for a gap year with the Lutheran Volunteer Corps. Working at a day shelter for homeless women in the nation's capital at the height of deinstitutionalization brought me into close contact not just with the most abject poverty but also schizophrenia and other forms of psychosis.

Thinking I wanted to be a journalist, reporting on Europe for Americans, I realized I needed much more of the history I had so far evaded and applied to and entered Brown University for graduate training. Initially, it was overwhelming, but also thrilling. And by the time I got the chance in my second year to be a teaching assistant leading discussion seminars for European intellectual history from Rousseau to Foucault, I was hooked. I was lucky to enter the discipline just as novel approaches to thinking about power, inequality, justice, and desire were being explored. And, by the time I was finishing my dissertation in the early 1990s (on Jewish rights, women's rights, and the dilemmas of liberalism in the nineteenth century), two new nascent subfields of history were just taking off: history of sexuality and history of the Holocaust. These, then, were also the foci of the classes I taught in my first posting after graduation, at Michigan State University.

This interest in topics that are extraordinarily morally and emotionally intense, contested, and complex, which raise myriad questions for which there are no easy answers but which allow me to learn new things from my students, year after year, about how they make sense of the world, has never left me. I feel fortunate that for now close to twenty years, the Graduate Center at the City University of New York – the largest urban public university in the country and a remarkable upward-mobility-machine for the immigrant working class – has been my home. Teaching is itself a kind of care work, and it remains, every day, a source of joy. I teach courses on the histories of gender and sexuality, fascism and genocide, disability and care, psychiatry and psychoanalysis, and interdisciplinary theory and historical method.

My books include: *Intimacy and Exclusion* (1996); *Sex after Fascism* (2005); *Sexuality in Europe* (2011); *Cold War Freud* (2017); *Unlearning Eugenics* (2018); and the forthcoming *The Question of Unworthy Life* (2024). My most recent coedited collection, with Chelsea Schields, is *The Routledge Companion to Sexuality and Colonialism* (2021). Although I am always trying to understand things that I couldn't comprehend before, there are evident recurring preoccupations. Among these are my search, in every instance, not just for documenting and explaining the far too many examples history provides of interhuman cruelty and complicity in evil, but also for recovering the idiosyncratic imperfect heroes and heroines in every location and era who found the sharpest counterarguments to injustices and inequalities of various kinds, or who simply modeled alternative ways of being. Looking for them, and always again finding them, often in utterly unexpected places, has taught me, over and over, that the past is an infinitely precious resource.

And here is an example of Dagmar's clear thinking and writing.

What is racism?

Racism is prejudice, antagonism, repression, or lethal harm directed at members of a group allegedly sharing inherited biological characteristics and deemed inferior and therefore not worthy of equal rights. Or put another way: Racism is a system of thought and feeling that has been evolved over centuries; it provides a framework for making sense of the world. It is rooted in a fiction, but it is a fiction with a vast array of material consequences.

Racism comes in two main forms. There is an exterminatory and exclusionary form (for example, settler colonial violence against Indigenous peoples in North America, Nazism's treatment of Jews, and also of Roma and Sinti), and there is a hierarchical and exploitative form (for instance, slavery across the Americas, Jim Crow in the U.S. South, apartheid in South Africa).

Structural racism is a crucial manifestation especially of the hierarchical and exploitative form. Examples of how it has manifested in the United States include: The long history of disenfranchisement at the voting booth (from terroristic violence to gerrymandering, voter suppression and now also voter substitution), dispossession of property through redlining and mortgage denial and "urban renewal" (and then disinvestment), and differential real estate valuing, the cultivation of systematic indebtedness, disproportionate incarceration rates, slashed budgets for public schooling, the placement of zones of environmental hazard. In other words, racism leaves its marks not only on hearts but also on – among other things – politics, labor, housing, health, and education.

What is fascism?

Fascism manifests as either an insurgent movement or as a dictatorial regime, but in either form it crystallizes around hostility to the values of liberty, equality, and fraternity. And by fraternity, I mean also: human capacities for empathy and solidarity. Fascism is always deeply hostile to empathy and solidarity; it organizes itself against those precious ideals. Fascism uses the law *against* the rule of law. It makes the judiciary useful to itself. It captures the legal system more generally so that legislatures and police and judges all enforce the movement's or the regime's desired divisions between who is "in" and who is "out," who is "up" and who is "down."

Fascism regularly relies on violence, or the threat of violence, and persecution, or the threat of persecution, removing political opponents from official positions, or imprisoning its enemies, or forcing them into exile. It can and will resort to assassination or execution of its adversaries and of targeted minorities alike. Nonetheless, it is never solely repressive, but deliberately channels also rebellious impulses – and then directs these into scapegoating the vulnerable and defenseless.

Fascism sees war as an opportunity, not a problem. It will wage war against outside enemies, engaging in a scorched-earth policy, brutal counterinsurgency, and lethal treatment of prisoners of war. In this way, fascism can represent the extreme radicalization of a nation's drive for colonial conquest and exploitation.

Yet fascism also involves knowledge control. This means both propaganda and censorship, and often, in addition, a demand for public displays of enthusiasm for the movement's or regime's leaders. And it frequently means inducements to denunciation – of neighbors, coworkers, even family members. Fascism is about turning citizens against each other.

Crucially, fascism is both nostalgic and aspirational. It appeals to an imagined lost greatness, and it promises a cleansing violence leading to renewal. It involves a nursing of grievances and resentments, and it stokes the fantasy of the group that wants to be dominant as pure and superior. Indoctrination is not so much into a set of ideas as into the conviction of in-group superiority.

There is, moreover, always a sexual politics to fascism. Fascism seeks to control reproduction and to intrude into privacy. It aggressively persecutes sexual or gender minorities, destroying families and chosen bonds in a way that (again) atomizes individuals. Take for instance the Nazis' Nuremberg Laws of 1935 which were all about determining who could have sex with whom and who could marry whom, and about calling into question the legal status of children of so-called "mixed" Jewish-gentile couples. More generally: All fascisms of the 1920s–1940s (that is, in Germany, Italy, Spain, Portugal) can be recognized by the fact that they were antiabortion and antihomosexual.

Not least: Fascism works to exploit the instability of truth. What counts as truth is always unstable and contested, but fascisms really revel in that dynamic. There is a kind of ecstatic rejection of reason, a gleeful indulgence in making outrageous claims, a habit of provocation and inversion of reality.

Imperfections in the would-be dominant group

Eugenics has played a starring role in the histories of both racism and fascism, but its emotional efficacy and its practical consequences remain far less well understood.

On the one hand, antidisability animus is without question another manifestation of *racial politics*. Its sharp contempt is almost always directed at perceived imperfections within the group that believes itself to be the legitimately dominant one. On the other hand, and not least because the vast majority of people deemed intellectually disabled or psychiatrically ill have historically come from the poorest strata of society, eugenics is at the same time a *class politics*. It is certainly a form of poverty management.

Eugenics was, like Nazi anti-Jewish propaganda, the "fake news" of its era. But it has been harder for historians to discern its falsity, if only because contempt for weakness and a feeling of superiority toward people with intellectual impairment can seem simply like a universally shared commonsense. And no doubt it is precisely the ambiguous status of people with cognitive or psychiatric disabilities – their uneasy positioning between a valued "us" and an abjected "them" – that helps to explain the force of disdain and ferocity to which they are so often subjected.

Eugenics was a transnationally influential movement in the 1910s–1930s, but the German case, in its very extremity and intensity, clarifies some key features of the broader phenomenon. In the Third Reich there was an especially intricate relationship, a peculiar synergy and complementarity, between "racial hatred" of the supposedly non-German and "racial fear" about the quality of Germans themselves – a fear that was given yet stronger impetus because of the humiliation of national defeat in World War I. What thus requires our attention – particularly for the years we can now recognize as a kind of incubation phase for fascism – is the convulsive fury directed not just at those increasingly categorized as outsiders (the idea that Jews were not German was, after all, another absurd fiction that took time and countless lies to create), but also against those *within* the Volk who were alleged to be defective. Already by the 1910s, arguments were being advanced that 1–2% of the German populace was not worthy of being allowed to reproduce ("permanently unsuitable for the production of offspring," as one physician opined in 1914). But, as noted, the wound to national pride inflicted by defeat in World War I lent heightened urgency to these speculations. By the 1920s–1930s, there were ever more phantasmagorical assessments circulating, of 10, 20, even 30% of the German population as being unworthy of reproduction. This was the context in which the Nazi state implemented a massive apparatus for curtailing the fertility of its own population.

Like other fascisms, Nazism worked through laws. The first "racial" Nazi law was passed in April 1933, driving "non-Aryans" – and anti-Nazis – out of government service. That affected officials and bureaucrats at every level, but also notaries, judges, teachers, professors. Individuals more willing or even eager to collaborate filled their places.

However, the second "racial" Nazi law was the coercive sterilization law, the Law for the Prevention of Hereditarily Diseased Offspring (*Gesetz zur Verhütung erbkranken Nachwuchses*), announced in July 1933. Notably, it was passed already two years before the Nuremberg Laws. This incrementalism was vital. The Nazis were worried about international optics; they attacked the weakest people first. And they knew that many U.S. states had sterilization laws, so they could present themselves as being in good company. International observers failed to notice that the Nazi law was distinctive in targeting the citizenry as a whole. Ultimately 400,000 individuals – women and men in approximately equal numbers – within the German Reich were coercively sterilized. It was not the 20 million sterilized of which some avid advocates had dreamed. But it was one out of every hundred human beings of reproductive age. No prior society had undertaken such a project. The number of sterilizations in the much larger geographic expanse of the United States was far lower.

Three points about this history of Nazi eugenics are especially significant:

- The assertions of "heritability" were totally threadbare. Physicians knew full well that the causes of "feeble-mindedness" or "psychopathic inferiority" were in most cases unknown. (Indeed, in the majority of cases, inadequate nutrition in conditions of poverty, fevers of toddlerhood untreatable in the era before antibiotics, or epilepsy before the rise of effective antiseizure medications were the primary determinants.) But the regime's experts went with assertions of heritability anyway and made pseudo-religious arguments about the need to have "faith" that this would strengthen the quality of the Volk. They recognized that it would take generations to make a difference, if ever, but that did not stop them from propounding their spurious claims. The official guidelines for doctors and judges issued by the regime's chosen experts expressly took up the problem that the hereditary transmissibility of intellectual deficits in a particular individual were generally impossible to prove. And yet and possibly precisely because of that, they instructed that

any scrap of potentially plausible evidence that a disability was "likely" to have had a hereditary component, was sufficient evidence to make a sterilization advisable, even mandatory.
- The classically fascist denunciation inducement was essential to the law's effects. In short, despite the flawed science underpinning the law, the vigor with which the notion that "feeble-mindedness" was hereditarily transmissible was promoted to the wider public as well as to every pertinent professional field, along with the eagerness with which experts across multiple societal sectors took up the framework provided by eugenics, turned what had been a concocted fabrication into something all too real. Reporting of candidates for sterilization was made compulsory. Remedial education teachers, social workers, religious charity institution directors, and doctors stepped up and complied. Fully one million people were proposed by their fellow citizens as potential candidates for sterilization.
- What the enthusiasm for eugenics shows is that the would-be dominant group was not and never is naturally dominant. The fantasy of being strong, healthy, beautiful, and smart was just that, a fantasy, a fantasy that was then implemented through brutality. As historian Gisela Bock aptly put it: "The promised 'race,' the 'master-Volk,' was not a given, it was not the real-existing German Volk, rather [the master race] had yet to be produced."

These remarks seem just as pertinent today, as we observe a new wave of neo-fascist and alt-right appeals to longings for supremacy and concomitant cruelty to the vulnerable sweep through otherwise democratic societies across the Western world.

By the fall of 1939, as the war against the outside began with the assault on Poland, the Nazis turned also to coordinating mass murder of people they deemed the most severely disabled. The ensuing "euthanasia" murders – in carbon monoxide-fueled gas chambers and mass shootings, through medication overdose, poisoning, and deliberate starvation – would overlap only partially with the coercive sterilization project as, on the whole, these two mass crimes against persons with disabilities targeted different subgroups. Nonetheless, as ever more historians have noted since the 1990s, particularly the early phase of gas chamber killings would come to function as a sort of "rehearsal" or "trial run" for a significant portion of the Holocaust of European Jewry as well. The big genocide and the little genocide were complexly interconnected.

Consequential fictions

The rise of eugenics had been multifunctional for its proponents. Vicious vilification of the disabled dressed up as the latest evidence-based serious scholarship served beautifully as distraction from the extensive collateral damage in a nation undergoing rapid industrialization. Eugenics diverted attention from the environmental destitution, unremediated socioeconomic inequities, and then-untreatable childhood ailments – from severe nutritional deficiencies to meningitis and encephalitis – that were the actual sources of the vast majority of mental disabilities. Its proponents and executioners blamed the victims instead, promoting the flawed premise that intellectual deficiency was biologically hereditary, when in fact it only looked that way because conditions of poverty had been replicating across generations. The wider public was fooled in part because all the fancy talk simultaneously provided flattering, cost-free ego boosts for those lucky enough to be deemed non-deficient. And then too there was – as one of the few astute contemporaneous critics noted – the "catnip" or "lure" that was repeatedly offered to those willing to join in the demeaning of the vulnerable as biologically defective: Doing so provided a rationalization for restricting social service spending. In sum, a eugenic framework offered readily available scapegoats and crudely simplified explanations to redirect popular anger at the unfairness of the world, while experts promoted the make-believe that eliminating welfare-care for "imbeciles" would mean that funds would be redirected to "worthier" families.

Fictions and fantasies are no less powerful for being rooted in falsehoods. Why is it so difficult to loosen their seductive holds? Thirty years ago, while delivering a triptych of talks at Harvard, the brilliant Jamaican-born British sociologist Stuart Hall offered a powerful answer to this puzzle. The comments may well have been made spontaneously in the Q&A, to elucidate a point, and did not make it into the final record of the lectures eventually published posthumously under the title *The Fateful Triangle: Race, Ethnicity, Nation*. But they are of lasting value. Hall had posed the rhetorical question: "If race is a social construct, why does racism persist?" Reply: "Because race is a social construct." In other words, if the would-be dominant group, in whatever geographical-political situation, truly were superior to the groups it was continually trying to treat as lesser, there would be no need for discussion. No need for elaborate conceptual frameworks. And no need for laws or violence, in order to make the hierarchies and exclusions, the subjugations and cruelties, seem justified.

Hall's insight could be taken as helpfully clarifying albeit hugely depressing. Yet we could also interpret the fragility of false certainties as giving us some optimism that positive change *is*, in fact, conceivable. This is so even when that positive change has been a very long time in coming, and has taken massive activist efforts to achieve – along with, notably, years of dedicated research by historians to uncover the past with greater accuracy so as to be able to counter the self-legitimating excuses, the twisting of facts, and the ongoing denigration of victims made by perpetrators and beneficiaries and those beholden to them.

Among the more striking documents that I have uncovered in my recent research is a "declaration of historical responsibility" promulgated by the Deutsche Gesellschaft für Humangenetik (German Society for Human Genetics) in 2008. The occasion was the 75th anniversary of the Nazis' 1933 sterilization law. The statement expressed the "heavy guilt" that lay on geneticists for "misusing their authority as scientific experts" in both formulating and implementing the law, and on the basis of "false premises" having participated in the "mutilation" of hundreds of thousands of fellow citizens. They even apologized for having continued to uphold eugenics notions after the Third Reich's demise. Among the statement's most poignant remarks is the observation that, "The behavior of the human geneticists [in the 1930s] is all the more incomprehensible as the biological absurdity of eugenics was obvious even with the level of knowledge of genetics at the time." In their concluding remarks, the geneticists dedicated themselves to "emphatic dissociation from any form of eugenic endeavors"; "respect for all people in their natural genetic diversity"; and the "rejection of any form of discrimination on the basis of ethnic characteristics or genetic disease or disability." Two years later, the Deutsche Gesellschaft für Psychiatrie und Psychotherapie, Psychosomatik und Nervenheilkunde (German Association for Psychiatry and Psychotherapy, Psychosomatics and Neurology) at long last followed suit. Its president, Frank Schneider, stood before 3000 of his peers and expressed "shame and sorrow" for the fact that it had "taken us so long" to acknowledge not just the involuntary emigration of Jewish and leftist colleagues, but also the substantial participation of psychiatrists in every aspect of the torment and killing of people with disabilities. He asked for forgiveness from "the victims of forced emigration, forced sterilization, human experiments, and murder."

Even though I know the countless hours and relentless determination it took on the part of historians to prompt and to prepare the groundwork for these formal declarations of apology, the fact that they ultimately did happen gives me great hope. Pernicious fictions can be undone.

Michael G. Hanchard
Racial Regimes, Here and Now

Our next reflection is written by Michael G. Hanchard. Michael and I first met at the University of Texas at Austin where we both held our first academic post-Ph.D. positions, Michael in Political Science, and I in German and Comparative Literature. We bonded quickly over the fact that we both hailed from Westchester County, New York, and that while doing his graduate work at Princeton, this Michael had known Michael Jimenez, someone I had met and hugely admired during my undergraduate days at Harvard while he was in a graduate program in History. Both Michaels were scholars of Latin America, Jimenez specializing in Colombia and Hanchard in Brazil. Michael Hanchard and I participated in an interdisciplinary reading group for several years in Austin where we read books that I'm not sure I would have been exposed to otherwise. I loved the different questions and perspectives the participants brought to bear on our discussions. Mike and I stayed in touch after he left for Northwestern and I, a year later, for Dartmouth. We have been able to share thoughts about the academy itself as well as about what makes for a good university work environment or not. I think Mike has taught me more about the reality of racism and the failures of U.S. democracy than anyone else. Some of what he knows about it and what he's taught me is in the piece he contributes to this volume.

But first, here's what he shares with us about himself:

My path to academia was a circuitous one, with several false starts and detours before finding myself on a secure track to the Ph.D. program in Politics at Princeton University. Before arriving at Princeton in the last years of the previous century, I worked for a while as a journalist and would-be writer, a pre-school teacher, security guard for a then well-known rock promoter, among other jobs which I knew were not my chosen path, but kept some income in my wallet and meager bank account. At some point during college, I decided that I wanted to make a living out of reading, thinking, and writing, a vocation and aspiration that distinguished me from most of my classmates at Tufts, who seemed more interested in corporate America. I was a 1981 graduate of Tufts with a degree in International Relations. But for most of my time there I was an indifferent student, often juggling a part-time job off campus, along with other responsibilities. I only made the honor roll during my senior year, and on a whim, in my last semester, I took a course with Professor Sol Gittleman on German Abstract Expressionism. In the mist of time, I cannot remember the exact requirements for the course, but I do remember completing an examination and turning it in, only to have the assignment returned to me the following week without a grade, and with a handwritten note from Prof. Gittleman that had two words "See me." Puzzled, nervous, I went to his office hours the following week. Did he think I cheated? Was my paper that bad? I walked into his office, not sure what to expect. He greeted me, and asked how I was doing. "Okay," I responded with a lump in my throat. "I have asked you in because I wanted to see who you are and get to know a little bit about you." He then looked down on his desk, and as I followed his gaze, I realized he was reviewing my student transcript. He then looked away from the transcript and asked me to pull out my exam. I gave him the two blue booklets. He paused, took a deep breath, and then said the following, "I wanted to get to know you because the person who wrote this exam can't be the same person with these grades on your transcript. This exam is simply brilliant. I think you are capable of doing what I do. Whatever else you do with the next few years of your life, remember that." I was stunned. Me? a professor, a scholar? After leaving his office, I told several of my friends. They could hardly believe it themselves. It took me a few years which included some of life's detours before I arrived on the path that led me to an M.A. degree at the New School for Social Research and then a Ph.D. from Princeton. That moment in Prof. Gittleman's office, in some fortuitous way, led me here . . . I am forever grateful to him and to many other superb scholars who took the time to mentor and teach me.

And these are the thoughts on racial regimes and democracy that Michael Hanchard shares with us.

My contribution here is a postscript of sorts to the argument I made in *The Spectre of Race: How Discrimination Haunts Western Democracy* (2018), as part of the conversation with historian Dagmar Herzog convened by Irene Kacandes at 1014. Space for Ideas in September 2022. Since my book's publication, the axial shift to authoritarian, even neo-fascist politics has occurred in many polities, some democratic, some not. What follows are more recent examples of racial regimes (aspirant and actualized) analyzed in my book and highlighted in my conversation with Prof. Herzog and the "Humanities for Humans" audience.

On December 7, 2022, the Special Forces of the German government announced the arrest of 25 people suspected of involvement in a plot to overthrow the German government in order to form, with constituents and collaborators, their own state. Those arrested included a judge in Berlin who was both a member of the far-right political party, Alternative for Germany (Alternative für Deutschland, AfD) and a former member of the German Parliament. Among the assorted coup plotters were a self-proclaimed prince and descendant of a former German royal family; members of elite police units, and former members of the German and East German armed forces; adherents to QAnon, fervent believers in the existence of a deep state and the necessity of its overthrow; and a far-right organization, the Reichsbürger (Citizens of the Reich). This last group believes that the post-World War II republic of Germany is not a sovereign state but rather a corporation created and administered by the victorious Allied Powers.

The group, which contained more members than the arrest of the first 25 people would indicate, had already formed a shadow government prepared to assume power after their hoped-for coup d'état. From surveillance, statements, and analysis of documents, the German government concluded that this group was prepared for armed struggle, which included the assassination of government representatives. According to *The New York Times*, *The Economist*, and several other international news sources, German intelligence services have concluded for years that the greatest threat to national security comes from domestic, far right extremist groups within Germany. A second, far-right plot to overthrow the German government was announced by the German government on January 16, 2023. The second plot was planned by five people, who were charged with treason. Their objective was to incite a civil war, abduct then public health minister Karl Lauterbach because of his anti-COVID health measures, and overthrow the government. Political assassinations were also part of their plan. According to news reports at the time, the second group was separate from the group uncovered one year earlier.[1]

Nearly two years earlier, on January 6, 2021, an insurrection that generated far more attention occurred in Washington, D.C.: the assault on the U.S. Capitol building, physical attacks upon members of several police departments, all part of a failed attempt to overturn the results of the U.S. 2020 presidential election.[2] This insurrection congealed before the entire world a range of political tendencies and incidents that had often been viewed in isolation from one another and seemingly, at a remove from mainstream U.S. politics: Charlottesville, Virginia in 2017; Kyle Rittenhouse in Kenosha, Wisconsin; and the plot to kidnap Michigan Gov. Gretchen Whitmer, the latter two both in 2020, to give three examples.

---

[1] "Five Charged over second alleged far-right plot against German government," AFP Berlin, Monday, January 23, 2023.
[2] For an insider account of the coordinated attack in the Capitol on January 6, 2021, and of the planning and strategizing leading up to the event, see embedded journalist and documentarian Nick Quested's film "Big Dose of Reality: 64 Days: The Insurrection Playbook" (2024), which focuses on Proud Boy leader Enrique Tarrio.

At his January 20, 2021 inauguration, president elect Joseph Biden declared, referring to the insurrection and the citizenry of the United States, "This is not who we are!" Well, Biden's comment begs the question, who is the *we* that President Biden was referring to?

Up until the insurrection, many citizens of the U.S. considered the Ku Klux Klan, the Proud and Boogaloo Bois, and similar contemporary organizations relics of a distant past or at best, extremist fringe political movements. What many students of U.S. politics failed to recognize was that these so-called fringe organizations were not anomalies in U.S. democracy, but occupants of U.S. democracy.

The emergence of exclusionary tendencies within democratic polities forces us to confront a seeming paradox: How could anti-democratic movements not only exist, but thrive in a democracy? Yet democracies, all the way back to classical Athens, have always tolerated some degree of inequality. For the Greeks, enslavement was considered a necessary institution, providing freedom for citizens to participate in the polis. In *The Promise of Politics* (essays mainly from the 1950s republished in 2005), Hannah Arendt suggests that freedom, the ability of citizens to participate in the Athenian polis, was made possible by the domination of slaves by members of the polis; "man could not be subject as a slave to someone else's domination, or as a worker to the necessity of earning his daily bread."[3] The "normal" functioning of the first democratic polis presupposed coerced labor.

Only if we understand how democracies function under "normal" conditions can we accurately assess whether democracies in the current epoch are under extraordinary or unusual strain. Actual democracies have never functioned in isolation from other political and economic orders – neither in the ancient world nor in our contemporary one. Oligarchy, which has a longer history than democracy, was defined as the politics of the rich. Democracy was defined by Athenians as the politics of the poor. Given this historical backdrop, we should especially view calls for a "return" to democratic political culture in popular and elite discourse with skepticism. They are misguided attempts to project democracy into the present and future based on false assumptions about democracy's past.

Karl Marx clearly understood the implications of the conjuncture of democracy and enslavement in the modern world when he declared in *Capital* that "to be free at home, (Britain) must enslave abroad." So did eighteenth-century commentators Edmund Burke and Adam Ferguson understand the implications. They warned that overseas empire would accelerate political and moral corruption in the liberal, democratic but no less imperial metropoles of Europe.

---

[3] Hannah Arendt, *The Promise of Politics*, Schocken Books, 2005, 116.

For those who have not read my study *The Spectre of Race*, what follows is a brief description of its contents. My book explores how the practice of democracy produces – and is affected by – political inequality. To take the first key theme, what I have called racial and ethno-national regimes are a combination of formal and informal institutions, laws and norms, combined with administrative and coercive practices implemented by governments and economies to systematically disadvantage certain groups, while providing advantages to members of dominant groups. Racial and ethno-national regimes have persisted in the world's most continuous democracies: France, Britain, and the United States, and in other nation-states both democratic and non-democratic.

The second key theme of the book is a recurrent tendency among some political actors and everyday folk in many national societies to assume that nation-states have – or should have – homogeneous populations. This has been a long-standing assumption, myth, and policy aspiration among nationalists in much of the nation-state system, according to which there should be symmetry between state and citizenry, whether in religious, ethno-national, or presumed racial terms. For example, Woodrow Wilson, the 28th president of the United States, details what he describes as "several all-important conditions" for the successful operation of democratic institutions.[4] Number one on his list is the:

> homogeneity of race and community of thought and purpose among the people. There is no amalgam of democracy which can harmoniously unite races of diverse habits and instincts or unequal acquirements in thought and action . . . A nation once come into maturity and habituated to self-government may absorb alien elements, as our own nation has done and is still doing . . . Homogeneity is the first requisite for a nation that would be democratic.[5]

At various points in the text, Wilson makes clear that even though U.S. Negroes, the brighter and more ambitious among them, have the capacity for self-government, they should never, under any circumstances, rule over the Saxon race, as was the case during Reconstruction.[6] In this same section Wilson does acknowledge that the United States had a history of absorbing "alien" populations into its society, mainly ethno-nationalities from central and southern Europe. Racial categorization provided Wilson and other adherents of Euro-Aryanism with a homogenizing device to render the diversity of European populations in the

---

4 Woodrow Wilson, *The Papers of Woodrow Wilson Vol. 2*, ed. Arthur Stanley Link, Princeton University Press, 1967, 74.
5 Wilson, *The Papers of Woodrow Wilson Vol. 2*, 74–75.
6 "Stray Thoughts from the South (22 February, 1881)," *The Papers of Woodrow Wilson Vol. 2*, ed. Arthur Stanley Link, Princeton University Press, 1967, 27. On this topic, see also Thulani Davis, *The Emancipation Circuit*, Duke University Press, 2022.

United States under a single, unifying chromatic rubric – whiteness–and to formulate a hierarchy of so-called races in a global order.

Let's pause to juxtapose Wilson's language just cited with the following excerpt from Adolf Hitler's speech in the *Reichstag* on January 30, 1937:

> . . . there is one error which cannot be remedied once men have made it, namely the failure to recognize the importance of conserving the blood and the race free from intermixture and thereby the racial aspect and character which are God's gift and God's handiwork. It is not for men to discuss the question of why Providence created different races, but rather to recognize the fact that it punishes those who disregard its work of creation.[7]

The conclusions of Wilson and Hitler, along with many contemporary politicians across the world, however, are based on faulty assumptions. The overwhelming majority of nation-states are constituted by a hodge podge of religious, ethno-national, linguistic, or presumed racial distinctions (please note the "presumed" in this sentence). This includes Germany which, in 1871, the year of its birth, consolidated an assortment of peoples that included Slavs, Franks, Saxons, Frisians among other nationalities and ethnicities. The idea of population homogeneity, just like classifications such as foreigner and citizen, is a political artifact, not something we find ready made in the world.

So many parts of the origin tales told by various ultra-nationalist and xenophobic movements in nation-states rely upon dangerous fictions, such as the need to create and maintain a pure, homogeneous population. But these fictions also help generate basic questions that involve questions of citizenship, the nation-state, and national belonging. Shall we let any of these outsiders in, and if so, which ones? By what criteria shall we include some people and exclude others? Once allowed in, who should be encouraged to leave, and who should be encouraged to stay?

As democratic institutions maintain barriers to civic membership, they must always justify their exclusions. Moments of geo-political crisis, such as that experienced by the Greeks during the Greco-Persian Wars, the era of the Red Scare in the United States, or the contemporary debate in the European Union regarding immigration and migration reveal popular and governmental anxieties about being overrun by certain – not all – foreigners. Citizenship becomes associated with particular types of people, and not the actual exercise of citizenship rights, duties, and responsibilities (*jus soli* versus *jus sanguinis*). This tendency is clearly in evidence in then President Donald Trump's January 2018 evocations of caravans ambling over the southern border of the United States filled with "danger-

---

7 Adolph Hitler, speech at the Reichstag, January 30, 1937.

ous criminals," principally from what he had referred to earlier as "shithole" countries.

There are many examples of authoritarian, populist movements and governments in the contemporary world who utilize the following chain of associations in their rhetoric: homogeneity produces national/state unity, political stability, and prosperity: Germany, Greece, Portugal, Austria, the Dominican Republic, Hungary, India, among others. Certain foreigners, people with distinct cultures, religions, sexual orientations, threaten this chain of associations.

The takeaway

So, what does all of this tell us about the practice of democracy in the current moment?

There is an ever-proliferating industry of books and articles on democracy's decline in the contemporary moment, much of which considers contemporary democracies as never in a more precarious state than they are in now. Yet democracies in practice have always contained what I am referring to as privileging design. Privileging design, through law, custom and the use of force, structures certain political, economic and social advantages to some groups and not others. The active presence of privileging design within democracies complicates our understanding of how democracies have actually functioned in the past, and as a consequence, our understanding of how they function in the present.

In his book, *The New Faces of Fascism*, historian Enzo Traverso notes a disquieting fact: the principal threats to the short-lived democracies of Spain, Italy, and Germany in the interwar period came not from exogenous movements but from within.[8] Democracies harbor their own precarities. In the 1920s and 1930s, opponents of democracy corroded its institutions and civic cultures, using notions of difference as a wedge to divide national populations. The same process is occurring now. The examination of racial and ethno-national regimes in democratic polities can serve as barometers of the health of plural societies. In order to do so, however, we must ask the following question: what price do democracies pay when they target and deny membership to certain groups based on criteria of ethno-national and presumed racial distinction?

I believe this question is important because racial and ethno-national regimes within democratic polities often rely upon democratic modes of deliberation, tactics, and strategy to maintain dominance by one group over one or more groups. Such

---

8 Enzo Traverso, *The New Faces of Fascism: Populism and the Far Right*, Verso, 2017, 4–5.

regimes require bureaucracy, intelligence (information gathering), and surveillance, often occult and hidden from the general population, to maintain a very particular public order. Abu Ghraib provides a contemporary example. Earlier examples include Japanese American Nisei internment during World War II, the Trail of Tears, and the expulsion of Chinese from the Pacific Northwest and California.

Historical coordinates and context

I want to offer some suggestions on how to think about our current moment in historical and comparative perspective, a pastiche of peoples, conflicts and circumstances across time and space: 1) white backlash in response to Reconstruction in the U.S. South; 2) the interwar years in Europe (1919–1929) and the rise of fascist states; 3) the relative inattention by the U.S. government to the proliferation of violent white supremacist groups. White supremacist reactions to the presence of Black people as political inhabitants of the state apparatus of the United States were evident in the visceral, negative reaction to Barack Obama's period in office. According to data compiled by the Southern Poverty Law Center, Obama's victory over John McCain triggered an increased proliferation of white supremacist, paramilitary groups across the United States. The Trump administration, along with Mitch McConnell and other members of the Republican party, sought no less than to erase the Obama presidency from the political history of the United States, as many Southerners did with Reconstruction.

In *The Anatomy of Fascism*, Robert Paxton has suggested that a U.S. version of fascism is not going to be an exact replica of what occurred during the interwar period in Europe, but it will share certain characteristics of earlier European fascisms as well as characteristics that are distinct to U.S. political culture. Paxton's observation is a provocation of sorts, and it has the advantage of forcing us to think comparatively about the similarities between fascism and what I am characterizing as racial rule. Paxton has suggested that the prototype for state fascism can be identified in the emergence of paramilitary forces in the U.S. South in response to Reconstruction to undermine federal authority, preceding Italian state fascism by over 60 years.[9]

---

[9] Robert Paxton, *The Anatomy of Fascism*, Knopf, 2005. One of the advantages of Paxton's account is its analytic distinctions between fascist regimes, fascist movements, and fascist states, allowing for nuanced comparison across cases and the disentangling of fascisms as political phenomena from the spaces and moments in which they operated. Ironically, Paxton suggests that

How does the U.S. government's reaction to Reconstruction and the targeting of Blacks for specific forms of terrorist violence at the end of the Civil War relate to the current moment? When Trump first took office, one of the earliest acts to signal the normalization of white supremacy in national politics was his removal of several white supremacist groups from the domestic terrorist watch list; in their stead, he had ANTIFA added to the list.

Despite the U.S.'s longstanding history of white supremacist violence, and white supremacist organizational increase during the Obama years, there has been very little data of public record provided by the intelligence community (IC) tracking violent white supremacist organizations and individuals since the Oklahoma City bombing committed by Timothy McVeigh and Terry Nichols in 1987. Between 1987 and the events of January 6, 2021, one unclassified document has been distributed by the Office of the Director of National Intelligence. The Office of the Director of National Intelligence released "(U) Domestic Violent Extremism Poses Heightened Threat in 2021" on March 1, 2021. The release into the public record of this document is significant for substantive and temporal reasons. Published three months after the aborted uprising at the U.S. Capitol on January 6, 2021, the document provides the following: "The IC assesses that domestic violent extremists (DVEs) who are motivated by a range of ideologies and galvanized by recent events in the United States pose an elevated threat to the Homeland in 2021. Enduring DVE motivations pertaining to biases against minority populations and perceived government overreach will almost certainly continue to drive DVE radicalization and mobilization to violence. (U) Executive Summary point 1)". Point 3 declares that in the assessment of the IC community, "racially or ethnically motivated violent extremists (RMVEs) and militia violent extremists (MVEs) present the most lethal DVE threats, with RMVEs most likely to conduct mass-casualty attacks against civilians . . . " Assessment 4: "US RMVEs who promote the superiority of the white race are the DVE actors with the most persistent and concerning transnational connections because individuals with similar ideological beliefs exist outside of the United States and these RMVEs frequently communicate with and seek to influence each other."[10] Thus, organizations and individuals motivated by white supremacist ideologies posed the most lethal threat to the do-

---

perhaps the earliest example of fascist forms of parallel regimes was the rise of the Ku Klux Klan and other racist, anti-Black organizations in response to Reconstruction.

For a discussion of the authoritarian policies of the Confederate government, Stephanie McCurry and Robert Mickey have provided historical evidence to suggest that the Confederate government was essentially an authoritarian regime during the Civil War.

10 "(U) Domestic Violent Extremism Poses Heightened Threat in 2021," Office of the Director of National Intelligence, United States of America, 2–3.

mestic security of the United States in 2021, with transnational linkages that trouble the distinction between domestic and foreign threats, and in turn, domestic and foreign policy.

At stake in the here and now, however, is not the mere sharing and dissemination of ideologies, but also of tactics, strategy, application, and deployment of techniques of violence surveillance, mass casualties, destruction, and crippling of infrastructure. The stakes are a rejoinder of sorts to President Biden's declaration cited at the beginning of this paper: unfortunately, in the United States and elsewhere, this is where WE are.

Several years ago, in a series of articles and lectures for the Institute for Advanced Study at Princeton, I wrote of the distinct possibility of racist violence, and, in turn, of popular resistance to that violence enacted in multiple, disparate skirmishes involving paramilitary groups, citizens who oppose them, and segments of the armed forces who would ostensibly show up to keep the peace by restoring "order." Barbara Walter's timely, sobering account *How Civil Wars Start* captures this possible scenario encroaching upon the political horizon of the United States.

Other possible sources of mobilization in the military and civil society warrant consideration. There are Black, Latino, Indigenous members of the armed forces who support Movement for Black Lives and allied groups, as well as soldiers who are opposed to such groups. Will this lead to dissension among the armed forces? As during the U.S. civil rights movement of the 1950s and 1960s, portions of the U.S. armed forces may be called upon to protect United States citizens from vigilante groups, and in so doing help salvage what is left of an already limited U.S. democracy. My concern here is not whether the label "fascist" in any form applies to the United States, or any other nominally democratic nation-state. Instead, I am demonstrating just one of several ways in which liberal democracies can be corroded from within, by ignoring the rot of racism within core nominally democratic institutions.

Many commentators have noted the rightward shift in global politics: the Alternative for Germany Party cited at the beginning of this essay, the Sons of Italy Party led by Prime Minister Georgia Meloni, the rightward shift in Sweden (Sweden Democrats) and Finland (Finns Party, and the National Coalition Party) respectively, and Modi's Hindu Nationalism in India.[11] As part of the right wing shift, each country has what on first glance would seem to be a highly restrictive, anti-immigration policy. But in many cases, policies of racialization are masquerading as immigration policy. In the Americas and the EU, racialized immigration policy

---

11 See Arjun Appadurai, "Modi's India Has Now Entered Genocidalism: The Most Advanced Stage of Nationalism," *The Wire*, January 10, 2022.

targets migrants from Africa, the Caribbean, and the Americas as unfit and unwelcome for entry, let alone citizenship and assimilation.

The rise of right-wing populism in many countries, with attendant attacks on "woke" culture and diversity, equity, and inclusion initiatives in several countries, has brought forth a sobering truth. What insurgent right-wing movements aspire to most is state power, authority, legitimacy, and majoritarian group dominance. Neither empathy, reconciliation, a politics of recognition nor mutual understanding are their goals. No less than the anti-colonial and nationalist struggles of the period after World War II, the process of desegregation in the United States required support from the U.S. armed forces, local and state police, and the National Guard. Remember the images of the National Guard and U.S. Army escorting the group of Black students known as the Little Rock Nine, in 1957? Let's be clear: the instantiation of full democracy in the United States required armed struggle or at a minimum, formal military supports. Kellie Carter Jackson's scholarship on the history of violence in the United States details how central the role of violence was to the Black freedom struggle as a form of collective defense against white domination.

Much media commentary and scholarship advocating anti-racist curriculum, education and political culture remains based on Enlightenment assumptions about defeating racism through education and socialization, fostering mutual understanding and empathy. Many of these pronouncements are based on wishful thinking, often citing a phrase by Martin Luther King that "the arc of history bends toward justice."[12]

If recent events in Germany, Brazil, the United States, Italy, India, and Israel are any indication, however, the bend in the arc of history needs structural support, or a nudge if you will, toward democratic deepening and repair. If we take a close look at how democracies have actually functioned, more often than not, barriers to political and civic membership of the formerly excluded have not fallen "due to some telos intrinsic to democratic politics; they fell, more often than not, because of the challenges made by those who were excluded."[13] Civil rights movements, feminist, abolitionist, suffrage movements demanded the incorporation of the formerly excluded into democratic polities. The dynamic relationships between movements seeking radical change and those who want to preserve the status quo in the current moment remind us, that democracy, not just electoral, but also social and economic democracy, is something that has to be fought over, often literally.

---

[12] See Michael G. Hanchard, "A Larger Pattern of Institutional Racism," *IAS, The Institute Letter*, Summer 2015, 1,17; "Democracy's Big Secret," *IAS The Institute Letter*, Fall 2020.

[13] Michael G. Hanchard, *The Spectre of Race: How Discrimination Haunts Western Democracy*, Princeton University Press, 2018, 107.

The wrong targets, or not guilty

As in the past, members of marginalized groups who have resorted to civil disobedience, marches, boycotts, sit-ins, even self-defense, are often identified as agents of terror, disorder, and mayhem. Abolitionists and suffragists in the United States, anarchists and trade unionists in Spain, Italy, Chile, and Germany are prime examples. Each group within their country and epoch was criminalized and, in some cases, jailed or murdered for their contestation of the limits placed on individual freedoms and popular participation in the polis, namely, the right to dissent. In the months leading up to the coordinated attack on the U.S. Capitol on January 6, 2021, some of the highest-ranking generals of the U.S. armed forces as well as intelligence personnel, stated publicly that the biggest threat to national security in the United States was what the CIA referred to as "Black Identity Extremists," with the Movement for Black Lives (formerly known as Black Lives Matter) as the allegedly primary example. What became immediately evident on January 6, however, was that the threat posed by white racist, neo-Nazi, and fascist organizations, encouraged by the former president of the United States, Donald Trump, was far more significant a threat to public order than the Movement for Black Lives. When compared to U.S. intelligence, German state intelligence more accurately identified the most immediate threat to its national security.

The focus of attention on the so-called Black threat within certain (not all) departments of the U.S. intelligence community and personnel and not the real threat posed by groups such as the Proud Boys and other populist authoritarian, white supremacist groups hints at the misdirection of certain sectors of the intelligence community and upper echelon military personnel in the United States. In the words of Stephanie LaRue, Chief of Diversity, Equity, Inclusion and Accessibility for the Intelligence Community, Office of the Director of National Intelligence, during a July 27, 2023 interview: "In the intelligence community, lack of diversity leads to bad intelligence."[14]

For example, it was revealed during the trial of Enrique Tarrio and other members of the Proud Boys on charges of sedition, that Mr. Tarrio was on the FBI payroll. His assignment? Provide intelligence on Black Lives Matter. So misdirected was the focus on the purported Black threat within certain sectors of the intelligence community that it led to inattention to documented evidence of plans to attack the Capitol in the weeks and days before January 6.

---

14 See also, "Spy Agencies Urged to Fix Open Secret: A Lack of Diversity," Associated Press online, Nomann Merchant, May 19, 2022.

There is at least one crucial commonality shared by the United States and Germany regarding the resurgence of anti-statist, racist, antisemitic, and xenophobic movements in both countries. Part of the reason why contemporary racist and fascist movements and ideologies resemble their counterparts from the 1930s through the 1940s is that those earlier ideologies, and their philosophical sediment, *never left*. Further, as in the 1920s and 1930s in Italy and Germany, people who sought to uphold democratic practices and to fight for the rule of law against arbitrary domination were – and are – criminalized.

Neither the Civil War in the United States, nor the fall of the Third Reich during World War II, eradicated the urge toward ethno-nationalism and state racism. Many key actors of the Confederate South and in the case of the Third Reich, leading scientists, thinkers and military leadership were incorporated into prominent positions in subsequent national governments, the judiciary and private enterprise. Many had not denounced their ideologies of white and Aryan supremacy. Here is where we can examine the United States and Germany as paradigmatic examples of incomplete consolidation, with implications for the contemporary moment. After the Civil War, state and local governmental authorities in the defeated south, with the help of several U.S. presidents such as Andrew Johnson and Woodrow Wilson, refused to provide material and ultimately military support to guarantee Black civil rights, and in fact encouraged paramilitary organizations such as the Regulators and most infamously, the Ku Klux Klan. Wilson supported the Klan's efforts to secure and maintain white racial rule. U.S. African Americans lived under a condition Hannah Arendt described as "apolity," circumstances under which people inhabit a territory without state protection.[15] My point here is that incomplete consolidation creates some of the political pre-conditions for localized sovereignties, and the basis for building larger-scale political orders. In the case of the United States, racial rule provides the embryo for nurturing fascist and authoritarian tendencies within a nominally democratic polity.

Democracy as a dynamic problem

In the chapter "Looking Forward," in his study *Black Reconstruction: An Essay Toward a History of the Part which Black Folk Played in the Attempt to Reconstruct Democracy in America, 1860–1880*, W. E. B. Dubois referred to democracy as a "problem," because it "expands and touches all races and nations." Regarding the relationship between enslavement and democracy in the United States, Dubois

---

[15] Hannah Arendt, *The Promise of Politics*, Schocken Books, 2005, 6.

posed the rhetorical question: "Was the rule of the mass of Americans to be unlimited, and the right to rule extended to all men, regardless of race and color, or if not, what power of dictatorship would rule, and how would property and privilege be protected?"[16]

Approaching democracy as a problem requires treating the concept as a stage for dynamic interactions involving institutions, ideas, norms, and people, and not a static ideal type. We can consider democracy as a mode of political community with prospects, rather than guarantees, of political equality.

Will the survival of democratic institutions ultimately rely upon the despotic exercise of state power to rid a polity and society of anti-democratic, anti-republican competitors and aspirants? What anti-democratic forces will be arrayed against contemporary (largely representative) forms of democracy? Will struggles for more egalitarian forms of political community, even more radical forms of democracy, emerge? Over the course of the twentieth and now twenty-first century, successive generations have sought to meld the multiplicity of human community – the fact of human pluralism – with egalitarian political institutions, practices, and culture.

I hope this brief commentary has provided a glimpse, if an uncomfortable one, of democracy's balancing act of egalitarian and unequal orders simultaneously. It is time for many of us to acknowledge that if democracy is to work at all, it must be made anew.

---

[16] W. E. B. Dubois, *Black Reconstruction: An Essay Toward a History of the Part which Black Folk Played in the Attempt to Reconstruct Democracy in America, 1860–1880*, First Edition, Harcourt, Brace and Company, 1935, vii.

Kathryn Abrams
On the Agency of Migrants

Of all the wonderful individuals who have contributed to this book, it is Kathryn Abrams I have known the longest. We met in our first year as undergraduates at Harvard or Harvard-Radcliffe College as our admissions letters read. Though we didn't become close friends at the time, we overlapped for many years in the Boston area during my graduate school years and Kathy's as an assistant professor of Law at Boston University. I will be forever grateful for contact with Kathy during those fraught years for me, since she not only generously helped me straighten out the mess of my first dissertation chapter, but she also helped me understand that I could get better at writing and that I shouldn't discount the talents I had as a teacher. We stayed in touch loosely as she went from one prestigious academic position to another. When I was asked to put together an issue for Women's Studies Quarterly *on the topic of "witnessing," I thought of Kathy immediately as someone I would like to collaborate with because of her extremely sharp intelligence, her wit, and her generosity that were already familiar to me. We collaborated felicitously on that project in a manner than she was not used to from her own discipline of legal studies, and that's why I thought of her right away for "Humanities for Humans."*

Here is what Kathryn Abrams shares with us about her intellectual journey.

For close to four decades, I have been a legal scholar, teaching and writing about inequality and civil rights. Although I've made my home at law schools – most recently, and happily, at UC-Berkeley Law School – I've always been a bit of an anomaly because legal doctrine and the courts that make it have never been the focus of my interest. I'm more interested in the lives of those whose equality has been denied or undermined through the force of law: how they talk about their experience and how they push back against their subordination. These efforts often highlight what has been excluded or marginalized within the formal legal record: resistance by individuals and by social movements. This resistance and the varied forms of agency that fuel it have been a through line in much of my work.

For many years I pursued this preoccupation in the field of gender. In the late 1980s I focused on the practice of first-person experiential storytelling, which was becoming prominent among feminist scholars. Despite the centrality of storytelling and narrativization in trials, as well as the sharing of first-person experience in contexts from rallies to legislative persuasion, storytelling in legal scholarship was new and almost immediately controversial. First person narration, with its affective charge, challenged the impersonality and dispassion that were unexamined aspirations for legal decisionmakers; its revelation of often-intimate detail breached the boundary between public and private, unsettling notions of scholarly decorum; its claim to knowledge grounded in tangible experience bucked the disembodied rationalism of the law. In "Hearing the Call of Stories" (1991), I sought to describe, analyze, and justify a practice that feminist and critical race scholars believed could stimulate new thought and argument within the law. This work fueled my interest in the agency of those living and working within systems of subordination, and how that agency might be fostered by collective action or social movement. I explored this interest through a case study, the "Sex Wars" of the early 1980s: a vivid intra-group feminist struggle over the legal regulation of pornography. For me, this conflict between feminists who decried the denial of sexual agency, and feminists who embodied its persistence and urged its centrality to political resistance, raised the question of how sexual agency and creativity might be possible within a culture that subordinated women's sexuality, and how collectivity or solidarity, such as that manifested by the feminist "sex radicals," enabled such expressions to flourish. My article, "Sex Wars Redux" (1995) traced the struggle and asked how the fragile but vital dynamics of "partial agency" – sexual agency specifically asserted within the confines of cultural, political, or legal constraint – might be cultivated in contemporary settings.

More than a decade ago, I became curious about studying social movements more directly. I wondered if I might learn more about the fostering of collective agency by moving from the library to marches, trainings, and actions of civil disobedience, and eliciting from activists directly the kinds of first-person narratives I had been studying. Surprisingly to me, the impetus for this move into qualitative empirical work was not a struggle over gender but over immigrant rights. In Phoenix, Arizona, "ground zero" of anti-immigrant state legislation and enforcement, a movement of undocumented youth and adults was organizing and mobilizing. This assertion of political agency by a group that was targeted and denied all incidents of membership struck me as remarkable. For five years, I watched and interviewed participants as they honed a series of practices that helped transform people who had lived below the radar of public visibility into outward facing activists who engaged the public and confidently made claims against the state and ultimately the nation. My recent book, *Open Hand, Closed Fist: Practices of Undocumented Organizing in a Hostile State* (2022), illuminates these practices and the surprising gains they made possible. The satisfactions of witnessing this transformation first-hand have been enormous for me. They have confirmed my interest in studying social movements, in their efforts to bring about legal and political change – an activity for which there is plentiful opportunity, given the retrenchment in many areas of the law governing equality.

My current project combines my interests in feminism and in social movements. I am studying reproductive organizing in abortion restrictive states, seeking to identify the factors that have made organizing across lines of race and class difficult, even in a time of escalated risk for a range of childbearing people.

And this is the further reflection on migration that Kathryn Abrams shares with us.

What images and assumptions shape our view of immigrants and asylum seekers? In asking this question, I focus on citizens of destination countries who begin with an attitude of receptivity toward migrants: who recognize their humanity, appreciate the enormous challenges they have faced, and support efforts to offer them safety and opportunity in our countries, even if we are not sure how that will occur. Unlike nationalist opponents of migration, these citizens of receiving nations do not intuitively conceive of migrants as a threat to our cultures, our economy, or our quality of life; their movement and aspiration do not demand the mobilization of a national defense.[1]

Yet even those who are presumptively well disposed toward migrants can rely on flawed assumptions in thinking about them and the qualities they bring to their new polities. In appreciating the vulnerability of migrants, or acknowledging what they have suffered through political oppression, economic collapse, or natural disaster, supporters in destination countries may see migrants exclusively as acted upon, rather than as actors in their own right. They may fail to glimpse the potentially generative forms of agency, that co-exist with this suffering, and persist despite the painful and constrained circumstances in which migrants have been placed. In the United States, this vision of unqualified migrant vulnerability has a long pedigree. The Statue of Liberty – Exhibit A in our case for ourselves as a "nation of immigrants" – bears the language of Emma Lazarus, which characterizes migrants not simply as "tired" and "poor," but as "huddled masses yearn-

---

[1] Of course, it is ultimately vital to persuade those who are opposed to migration as well. It is possible that highlighting the agency of migrants – which points to the range of their contributions to receiving countries – may play a role in moving them toward a more receptive attitude. But, if one takes seriously their public rhetoric, nationalist and other anti-immigrant actors tend to conceive of migrants – at least in the aggregate – as too powerful, rather than as lacking in agency. In part for this reason, I focus this argument on the assumptions of the more receptive. I also find it surprising that those who hold receptive attitudes toward immigrants may harbor assumptions about them that are potentially stigmatizing and counterproductive.

ing to breathe free" and as "wretched refuse" of other nations' "teeming shores." Not only does this vision glorify as beneficence forms of support that should be regarded as a basic human entitlement; but such largesse seems to be inevitably coupled with the abjection of those migrants who receive it. Such abjection is often sharply at odds with what we see in the lives of migrants, whether immigrants, refugees, or asylum seekers. In this essay I will explore the agency that can be observed in varied circumstances of international migration. I will ask what it portends for our treatment of migrants that many who support their struggles fail to see such agency.

The political agency of undocumented residents

I first had cause to reflect on this image when I began to study a group of undocumented immigrants who were long-term residents in the United States, living in the immigrant-hostile state of Arizona.[2] My attention was drawn to Arizona around 2010, when the state's passage of what was then the most hostile cluster of anti-immigrant laws in the nation culminated in its "show me your papers" statute, which authorized state and local law enforcement to demand the documents of anyone they suspected of being present without formal legal status. The new law had the predictable – and intended – effect of prompting tens of thousands of people to leave Arizona for their countries of origin or more welcoming states. But it also had the less predictable effect of fueling a new movement for the rights of undocumented people. Over the course of five years, I observed undocumented activists of all ages, working collectively to transform themselves from people living fearfully below the radar screen of public visibility to confident and knowledgeable political participants. These emerging activists not only served as the public face of a targeted community; they also developed strategy, made demands on state actors, and engaged with their fellow citizens on the substance of immigration policy. While political agency is not the only form of agency manifested by America's undocumented residents – examples of economic initiative and civic contribution also abound – it may be the most striking because it has emerged without the usual foundation of formal legal status.

---

2 This research formed the basis of my book, *Open Hand, Closed Fist: Practices of Undocumented Organizing in a Hostile State*, University of California Press, 2022.

One of the ways that immigrant activists pressed their agenda was to become involved in democratic, specifically electoral, processes.³ Although, as non-citizens, undocumented immigrants could not exercise the franchise, they could register and mobilize voters for candidates or policies that advanced their security or opportunity in the state or the nation. One of the earliest such efforts was a 2012 campaign called "Adios Arpaio," led by an organization that educated and engaged immigrant youth and supported by other organizations of undocumented immigrants throughout the Phoenix area.⁴ This campaign aimed to unseat the virulently anti-immigrant sheriff of Maricopa County, Joe Arpaio, by mobilizing Latino voters, many of whom had been "low propensity voters" in the past. Adios Arpaio employed the distinctive strategy of utilizing undocumented youth to educate, register and activate prospective voters. By engaging voters at their doorsteps, and explaining in concrete autobiographical terms the personal costs of Arpaio's enforcement practices, young activists aimed to persuade Latino voters that their mobilization was essential and could defeat the sheriff who terrorized immigrant communities. Although these efforts did not unseat Arpaio on the first try – they did on the second, in 2016 – activists in this initial effort registered more than 50,000 new voters. Observing the young canvassers knowledgeably explaining the electoral process and the stakes of the vote, citizens learned something beyond the importance of their own franchise. They learned that immigrants, whom they previously might not have seen as active contributors to their community, were invested, organized, and agentic: they could deploy strategic, logistical, and human resources to accomplish a goal, like the citizens they aspired to be.

A display of political agency on an even larger scale took place a decade later. Among the anti-immigrant laws Arizona enacted in the first decade of this century was a ballot issue that denied undocumented students in-state tuition at state universities. Though the law had been struck down by a lower (state) court after the announcement of DACA, and though the trustees of the state university voted to provide in-state tuition to DACA recipients, that lower court decision had been invalidated by the state Supreme Court. A large team of affected students, mobilized by an organization led and staffed by undocumented immigrants, learned and utilized the skills of legislative advocacy.⁵ Their efforts persuaded the state legislature to place on the ballot Proposition 308, a referendum calling for in-state tuition for

---

3 This process, and the "Adios Arpaio" campaign in particular, are discussed in Chapter 3: Abrams, *Open Hand, Closed Fist*, 74–94.
4 The organization leading the Adios Arpaio campaign was Promise-Arizona, which worked in partnership with the political action committee of the hospitality union, Unite Here.
5 The labyrinthine process of seeking in-state tuition, and the beginning of the legislative campaign of Aliento, which organized the students, is discussed in *Open Hand, Closed Fist*, 190.

undocumented students.[6] Then statewide efforts by immigrant organizations and allies to mobilize the vote led to a landmark victory at the polls.[7] Once again, citizens witnessed the focused intention and acquired skills of undocumented students who had learned to advocate on their own behalf, for the higher education that would allow them to make skilled contributions to the polity and economy.

What facilitated this agency? First, publics accustomed to the privilege of citizenship often ignore the fact that the decision to leave one's familiar social, geographic, and cultural landscape for an unfamiliar and uncertain future itself pre-selects for a strong sense of agency. Migrants' initiative, planning, and persistence in the face of unanticipated hardships can be substantially lost, even erased altogether, amidst the narratives of squalor, exploitation, and sheer numerosity that frequently accompany media coverage of migration. This is one reason that immigrant youth – during the 2013–14 campaign for Comprehensive Immigration Reform – coined the slogan "Our Parents Were The Original DREAMers." This effort sought to demonstrate to a public who would be asked to confer a path to citizenship on undocumented adults as well as youth, that the qualities of initiative, creativity, and persistence so often ascribed to DREAMers (undocumented immigrants brought to the U.S. as children) were characteristic of their parents as well.[8]

Beyond this initial endowment, undocumented activists learned to cultivate agency – both individual and collective – by making visible those resources each person already possessed and fortifying them through the support and solidarity of a community. One example is the practice by many undocumented organizations of treating one's "story" – a personal narrative about experience as an immigrant – as a resource to be utilized by both the individual and the collective.[9] Sharing stories within organizations helps new participants to see the combination of constraint, initiative, and small steps forward that characterize each of

---

[6] Proposition 308 provided that any student who had been resident in the state for at least two years and had graduated from an Arizona public, private, or home high school, regardless of immigration status, was eligible for in-state tuition and state financial aid. Arizona Proposition 308: In-State Tuition for Non-Citizen Residents Measure (2022). https://ballotpedia.org/Arizona_Proposition_308,_In-State_Tuition_for_Non-Citizen_Residents_Measure_(2022).

[7] Rafael Carranza, "Arizona Prop 308: 'Dreamer' Tuition Measure Passes as Final Votes Tallied," *Arizona Republic*, November 8, 2022. https://www.azcentral.com/story/news/politics/elections/2022/11/08/arizona-proposition-308-election-results-undocumented-students-tuition/8247766001/.

[8] For the trajectory of this argument, grounded in a sincere and oft-repeated belief of immigrant youth, is described in Dara Lind, "DREAMers' Parents Aren't Protected in Immigrant Plan Their Kids Fought For." *Vox*, December 1, 2014. https://www.vox.com/2014/11/25/7277027/dreamers-parents-arent-protected-by-the-immigration-plan-their-kids.

[9] The role of storytelling in the undocumented immigrants' movement is described in Abrams, *Open Hand, Closed Fist*, 49–62.

their lives. The familiarity of these patterns and the sense of possibility they often suggest also help to build bonds among immigrant activists that bolster them in the often-daunting turn to public visibility. New participants also learn that their stories are resources outside the organization, through which they can engage the attention of lawmakers and the public, humanize and concretize the claims of their group, and forge the kind of momentary personal connection that can change minds and turn bystanders into supporters. Finally, undocumented activists come to recognize that their community, which may lack in material wealth, has other resources that can be transformed into political strengths: from informal networks that facilitate communication and mobilization, to access to Spanish language media, to cultural histories of protest, to the experience and support of Chicano activist allies.[10] They learn that solidarity and mutual support from other organizational members can function as an antidote to fear.[11] And they witness the ways in which participation in the institutional and extra-institutional processes of political persuasion – from electoral canvassing to legislative advocacy to direct action and civil disobedience – can become self-reinforcing activities, through which the experience and knowledge gained generate an internal sense of authorization and sometimes an external perception of contribution-based belonging.[12]

The fugitive agency of migrants on the move

Analyzing the sources of agency among longtime undocumented residents makes clear the greater challenges of asserting agency for migrants who have not yet arrived at their destination. Far from being long-time residents, they are not (yet) part of a community and may lack even a reliable temporary home. Asylum seekers may remain outside, at the threshold, or perpetually in transit toward, the countries in which they hope to reside. Denizens of refugee camps live in but are not "of" those countries in which they temporarily reside: they cannot predictably build de facto ties to surrounding economies, nor draw on educational or civic institutions to develop cultural ties. Seasonal workers may labor in harsh

---

[10] The recognition and use of these community-based resources by the undocumented immigrants' movement is described in Abrams, *Open Hand, Closed Fist*, 28–39.
[11] For a discussion of undocumented organizers understanding and management of emotions such as fear and solidarity, see Abrams, *Open Hand, Closed Fist*, 62–73.
[12] The effect of these forms of participation on the political consciousness of undocumented activists is discussed in Abrams, *Open Hand, Closed Fist*, 169–183.

and precarious conditions, their sole tie to their host country being the employer who often exploits their precarity. For all these groups, the circumstances of being perpetually or episodically in transit, of living in temporary encampments or quarters, of being separated by often-arbitrary bureaucratic processes from their fellow travelers, make it challenging to develop bonds to each other that can fuel collective agency or empower individuals. And the immediate circumstances of extreme hardship – the malnutrition, illness, or injury that arise for many from a long and treacherous journey; the demands of navigating an obscure, arbitrary, and shifting system of eligibility and processing; the challenge of day-to-day existence in crowded, unhealthful, inhumane conditions – appear calculated to sap initiative and agency to an unprecedented degree.[13]

Yet even under these conditions, scholars, relief workers, and others in immigrant-focused NGOs have begun to shine light on striking examples of individual initiative and collective self-assertion. This is often a fugitive agency: if time allows, it may build or develop self-reinforcing dynamics. But it may as often pass, or recur intermittently, depending on the circumstances in which it emerges. To begin with an example of comparative stability, consider the activities of residents of the Za'atari Refugee Camp in Jordan. This camp, the world's largest for Syrian refugees, is home to an estimated 80,000 people. Although most residents of the camp hope to return to Syria, and virtually none can obtain permits to work in Jordan, the camp, as highlighted by a report of the Oxford Refugee Study Center,[14] reflects a complex blend of transience, stasis, and – more surprisingly – generative agency. In many ways, the refugees who have made Za'atari their temporary home have sought to re-create features of their home communities and have collectively engaged the aid groups that serve the camp. The refugees' agency fuels an informal economy and nascent civil society institutions. The "Shams Elysées," a blocks-long market street, houses hundreds of refugee-run shops and stands. Growing teams of audio, print, and online journalists reflect on their experience in extended transition, cover events at Za'atari, and introduce residents to the aid agencies operating throughout the camp. Residents of the camp have also acted collectively to contest some choices made by those aid agencies in administering the camp. This resistance is sometimes indirect, as when residents disassembled tents constructed for them and began to move them – with the help of entrepreneurial "removal men" –

---

[13] It is also more difficult for scholars or journalists to observe the lives of these groups, because they may be perpetually on the move, or because they are being maintained in settings to which neither members of the public nor media have regular access.

[14] Alexander Betts, Louise Bloom, and Nina Weaver, *Refugee Innovation: Humanitarian Innovation that Starts with Communities*, University of Oxford Refugee Study Center, 2015. The examples discussed below are described at 17–24.

to new locations that brought them into proximity with extended family or replicated their previous neighborhoods. This contestation is sometimes more direct: as when residents successfully sought the provision of cash, or cash equivalents, to buy food at camp-based markets, in place of agency-provided food, which they judged to be subpar. Aid agencies are not always receptive to these assertions of refugee agency.[15] But it reflects residents' persistent will to establish recognizable forms of collectivity and to shape the material circumstances of their lives, notwithstanding their transience and the structural constraint they inevitably confront.

Even in the chaos of migrant movement from one site or jurisdiction to another, social scientists have documented the emergence of improvised forms of individual and collective agency. Anthropologist Synnove Bendixsen, studying migrants traversing the Balkans en route to Western Europe, explores the elaborate, if informal, collaborations among migrants seeking information, strategy, and assistance, as they negotiate a rapidly changing labyrinth of border regimes.[16] She describes the often-collective process that migrants call "going on the game" – or figuring out how to get to the next stop. This process transpires in parks or other unofficial sites, as migrants "exchange information about the routes and recommendations about which EU country to head for, build networks, contact networks of smugglers, rest, and plan the next stage of the journey."[17] Anthropologist Cristiana Giordano also identifies intense, collective, informal activity among migrants, specifically among transient agricultural workers in Italy.[18] Surveying an old airport structure, now repurposed as a migrant welcoming and processing center, Giordano finds a hole in the fence surrounding the structure, on the other side of which migrants have created a "vast shantytown, bristling with activity of

---

[15] As one researcher quoted in the Betts report noted, "I was struck by the ingenuity and agency these Syrians [the refugees living in the camp] were expressing. My sentiment was not entirely shared by the NGO staff." Betts, Refugee Innovation, at 18. See generally, Suraina Pasha, "Developmental Humanitarianism, Resilience, and (Dis)Empowerment in a Syrian Refugee Camp," *Journal of International Development* 32 (2020), 244–259, explaining how Jordanian state priorities and the role played by international aid organizations "incrementally unwound and stifled refugee self-governance structures and informal entrepreneurialism."
[16] Synnove Bendixsen, "Journeys Interrupted: The Labyrinthine Border Experience Along the Balkan Route," *Continental Encampment: Genealogies of Humanitarian Containment in the Middle East and Europe*, eds. Are Knudsen and Kjersti Berg, Berghahn Books, 2023, 190–215.
[17] Bendixen, *Journeys Interrupted*, 205.
[18] Giordano's research at this site is reported in Cristiana Giordano and Greg Pierotti, *Affect Ethnography: Exploring Performance and Narrative in the Creation of Un-Stories*, Bloomsbury Academic, 2024, 159–165.

all sorts."[19] She describes "people, bicycles, animals, merchandise, food" all passing through this hole in the fence.[20] "The shantytown was immense," Giordano notes, "and offered all sorts of access to goods, services, social interactions, and exchanges that the fenced and guarded area did not allow."[21] This flurry of activity, taking place under the "knowing but indifferent"[22] gaze of law enforcement agents, proved so (comparatively) profitable that some agricultural workers Giordano spoke to had left their jobs to devote themselves full-time to this informal economy. Giordano analyzes this site as "a space of disorientation where the inside and outside of the reception center and the shantytown are blurred and unmappable" and as a "'collaboration' among the institution and the informal world."[23] But it is also a site where an unquenchable agency – a will to create and thrive – finds expression.

Vulnerability, agency, and migrant futures

Depicting migrant vulnerability in the Emma Lazarus register may have a certain appeal to lawmakers, particularly in the United States. To a degree that has become controversial, justifying intervention by the American legal system (for example, in the sphere of civil or human rights) has often rested on a depiction of vulnerability or imposed incapacity among prospective beneficiaries.[24] From the "discrete and insular minorities" whose isolation and stigmatization justify judicial intervention under the Constitution[25] to the women and children whose vulnerability has often served as a warrant for legislation, depictions suggesting an absence or a thoroughgoing destruction of agency have often been understood as the cost, or at least the currency, of legal intervention.

This approach is shortsighted in several ways. It positions legal or political actors as acting from beneficence: from a kind of *noblesse oblige* of citizens

---

19 Giordano and Pierotti, *Affect Ethnography*, 161.
20 Giordano and Pierotti, *Affect Ethnography*, 161.
21 Giordano and Pierotti, *Affect Ethnography*, 161.
22 Giordano and Pierotti, *Affect Ethnography*, 161.
23 Giordano and Pierotti, *Affect Ethnography*, 163–164.
24 This has been a particularly contentious issue in the field of domestic or intimate violence. See, for example, Martha Mahoney, "Legal Images of Battered Women: Redefining the Issue of Separation," *Michigan Law Review*, 90 (1991), 1–94.
25 United States v. Carolene Products, 403 U.S. 144, 152–53 n. 4 (1938). This understanding of the basis for judicial intervention under the Constitution was famously elaborated in John Hart Ely, *Democracy and Distrust: A Theory of Judicial Review*, Harvard University Press, 1980.

whose "birthright lottery"[26] endowed them with secure and prosperous homes. It reflects a refusal to acknowledge the arbitrariness of this initial endowment and a view of migrant-welcoming policies as supererogatory, making them subject to change or full withdrawal as the costs of such beneficence escalate. Democratic mayor Eric Adams of New York City once welcomed migrants from the border, declaring that "[there is no place for you here] is wrong ... that is not who we are as a city, and that's not who we are as a country."[27] Adams, however, reversed course as the influx continued, stating apocalyptically that the migrant "crisis" will "destroy New York City."[28]

Importantly, currently dominant migrant narratives may prove shortsighted from the perspective of migrants as well. Undocumented immigrants who have utilized experiential stories as a longtime strategy for eliciting emotional engagement among members of the public, have begun to wonder whether the vulnerability disclosed in such stories is an unnecessary concession to the sensibilities of citizens or an invitation to re-traumatization. "How much more do we have to keep catering to the privileged ones who don't get it, in order for them to get it?" one organizer asked me toward the end of my research in Arizona, explaining: "it's like we're putting [ourselves] naked in front of [them] ... People shouldn't feel like they have to or they need to."[29]

To depict agency on the part of migrants, on the contrary, may enable citizens to see migrant integration as producing generative opportunity for both the aspiring members and the receiving polity. The receiving country experiences the benefits not only of economic productivity and entrepreneurialism – gains the public and private sectors have been quick to see in the case of knowledge workers and other economically privileged migrants but less so in the case of poorer migrants, whether immigrants or asylum seekers. It may also see gains in civic engagement and investment, in appreciation of the virtues of institutions that longtime citizens in the U.S. or Western Europe may have come to view with cynicism or suspicion. Migrants too may be more comfortable with such depictions. Another Arizona activist shared that her emotional response to her own narra-

---

26 See Ayelet Shachar, *The Birthright Lottery: Citizenship and Global Inequality*, Harvard University Press, 2009.
27 "Transcript: Mayor Adams Hosts Rally and Delivers Remarks Calling for Expedited Work Authorization for Asylum Seekers," NYC (Official Website of the City of New York), August 31, 2023. https://www.nyc.gov/office-of-the-mayor/news/628-23/transcript-mayor-adams-hosts-rally-delivers-remarks-calling-expedited-work-authorization.
28 Emma Fitzsimmons, "In Escalation, Adams Says that Migrant Crisis 'Will Destroy New York City,'" *New York Times*, September 7, 2023, https://www.nytimes.com/2023/09/07/nyregion/adams-migrants-destroy-nyc.html.
29 Abrams, *Open Hand, Closed Fist*, 201.

tion varied, depending on whether it was intended to conjure vulnerability or agency. In storytelling to citizens, where activists often shared their pain to prompt empathy and action, "it made me go into a victim mode"; whereas when she told her story at meetings of undocumented people, where her message aimed to build capacity, it summoned more of a feeling of "we can do this."[30]

We must be wary of depicting heroic agency, a vision of migrants as a group of unremitting strivers whose success or commitment can set a new bar for stalled economies or eroding democratic commitment. This kind of trope, reminiscent of "model minority" imagery, can set migrants against domestic racial or ethnic minorities or perpetuate a practice of contrasting "good" with "bad" immigrants.[31] This view of heroic agency can also encourage lawmakers or the public to overlook the intolerable constraints and conditions to which migrants are often subject, or exacerbate the "bootstrap" mentality that inflects many Western cultures and is a particularly dominant thread in American individualism.

The goal should be, rather, to depict migrants – and free migrants to depict themselves – as full human beings, who can be blighted by oppression and violence, be riven with fear or fatigue, *and also* be fueled by will and aspiration, capable of invention and resilience that may reassert themselves, with even modest opportunities. This view of complex, multi-faceted humanity can buttress a regime that sees migrants as broadly entitled to opportunity and support.

---

[30] This interview is discussed in part in Abrams, *Open Hand, Closed Fist*, at 200. In neither of these settings, however, did this activist feel that storytelling contributed to her healing from the trauma she had suffered by being stopped by police and temporarily placed in deportation proceedings.

[31] Scholars have questioned both the strategy and the effects of dichotomizing immigrants in this way. See, for example, Abigail Andrews, "Moralizing Regulation: The Implications of Policing 'Good' Versus 'Bad' Immigrants," *Racial and Ethnic Studies*, 41.14 (2018), 2485–2503.

Part Two: **Assessing the Stakes**

Bruce Robbins
Equality in (Our) Time

One of what I consider the immense privileges of academic life is the ability to build a broad network of interlocutors through colloquies that take place in many locations. Long before we began to find each other so easily through the internet, academics met at seminars and conferences to share research, with breaks and meals providing opportunities to further exchange ideas and to get to know one another as people. Bruce Robbins and I first met at a meeting of progressive left-leaning professors convened by Stanley Aronowitz in New York City in the early 1990s. We just happened to be seated next to one another and when Bruce asked my name, he started speaking flawless Greek to me. Between our politics, our academic fields, and our connections to Greece, we were always happy to bump into one another, most frequently at the annual meetings of the Modern Language Association. Bruce helped me and my career concretely as a reviewer of my promotion dossier and supporter of the risk I took in writing my study of my paternal family's experiences during the Fascist Occupation of Greece, Daddy's War, *in an experimental fashion. (One only finds out about such support after the fact because these kinds of evaluations are highly confidential while they are happening and are forever kept so in most private universities.) More recently we laughed over a very negative critique he gave of one of my early articles – you didn't think I would like this, did you? – something I had forgotten until I unearthed it recently, while finally going through decades-old files.*

This is what Bruce Robbins shares with us about his intellectual journey.

To be honest, I didn't pursue a graduate degree in hopes of changing the world. Like so many other young people in the late 1960s and early 1970s, I did want to change the world. But all that was vague, atmospheric, a matter of marching in occasional demonstrations. What I could see right in front of me was the absolute need to make a living and the desire to do so while having an interesting time, if possible. Also, in a time of war, I was eager to do no harm, again, if possible. Inequality was present to my mind, but present in a complicated way. My parents had not been to college, and when I got to Harvard, that put me in an embattled minority, competing with other students who had major cultural advantages. What spurred me on was the desire to compete and do well, as my parents had, not a desire for equality. It was only when I started work on my dissertation that my identification with my grandparents kicked in. They had had no education at all. One grandfather had died in an industrial accident. My grandmother had come to America to escape life as a servant. I wrote my dissertation and my first book about servants.

I wrote that dissertation while living in Europe and considering the prospect of exile – or expatriation, if I chose to consider life in Europe a choice rather than an accident. I was inspired by Edward W. Said's writings on exile as a model for the intellectual. The next books I wrote (back in the U.S. by then) were about intellectuals, professionalism (seen as a defensible career choice even on the left), and cosmopolitanism. I addressed cosmopolitanism first of all as distance FROM nationalism and militarism, but also as a vehicle for global economic justice. It's at this point that economic equality came back to the fore for me.

I teach in the department of English and Comparative Literature at Columbia University, where I am proud to be able to sign myself as Old Dominion Foundation Professor of the Humanities – a title once held by Edward W. Said. My most recent books are *Atrocity: A Literary History* (forthcoming in 2025), *Criticism and Politics: A Polemical Introduction* (2022), and *The Beneficiary* (2017). My other books include *Perpetual War: Cosmopolitanism from the Viewpoint of Violence* (2012), *Upward Mobility and the Common Good* (2007), *Feeling Global: Internationalism in Distress* (1999), *Secular Vocations: Intellectuals, Professionalism, Culture* (1993), and *The Servant's Hand: English Fiction from Below* (1986). A collection of essays entitled *Cosmopolitanisms*, co-edited with Paulo Horta, came out in July 2017. I have also edited *Intellectuals: Aesthetics, Politics, Academics* (1990) and *The Phantom Public Sphere* (1993) and co-edited, with Pheng Cheah, *Cosmopolitics: Thinking and Feeling beyond the Nation* (1998) and (with David Palumbo-Liu and Nirvana Tanoukhi) *Immanuel Wallerstein and the Problem of the World* (2011). My essays have appeared in *The Baffler*, *n+1*, *The Nation*, *The New Statesman*, *Public Books*, the *London Review of Books*, and the *LA Review of Books*.

My organized efforts on behalf of the Palestinian cause began in 2002, when I collaborated (with the physicist Alan Sokal) on an "Open Letter of American Jews to Our Government," that called for cutting off all American aid to Israel if Israel would continue not to recognize the relevant United Nations resolutions. The "Open Letter" was published in the *New York Times* with over 4000 signatures, translated around the world, and re-published in 2006.

In 2014 I was co-proposer of Modern Language Association Resolution 2014-1, calling on the U.S. Department of State to contest Israel's denials of entry to the Palestinian West Bank to United States academics who have been invited to teach, confer, or do research at Palestinian universities. The resolution gained the support of an overwhelming majority, 1500 of the 2500 votes cast, though the required 10% of members did not vote.

I am also the director of a documentary entitled "Some of My Best Friends Are Zionists," available at bestfriendsfilm.com, and another called "What Kind of Jew Is Shlomo Sand?" available at Mondoweiss.

And here is what Bruce Robbins shares with us. I include the date on which he drafted it, as that date's proximity to the events of October 7 might be of interest to readers.

October 16, 2023

These days we academics, among others, are talking with more ease and enthusiasm about equality, and that's a good thing. Not long ago, talk of equality was a bit awkward, a bit constrained. People saw the virtue of it, but they were hesitant to hold that banner too high as they marched in one cause or another. The social movements of the 1960s suspected that demanding equality was not enough; maybe equality was even the wrong thing to demand. Like other social movements, so-called "difference" feminism looked, at least from the outside, as if it were suspicious of any and all universal norms, including equality, on the grounds that such norms were masculine, false universals, willfully blind to the essential and irreducible differences between categories of people, like men and women. Any supposedly common standard always implicitly favored one side over the other, so its results were biased. Quantification, the most blatant standard of measurement, seemed self-evidently to be a mistake. Any quantification of injustice was itself an injustice.

On these issues, "difference" feminism lined up against "equality" feminism, which was more concerned with measurable matters like equal pay for equal work. Another way the battle lines were drawn (notably by philosopher Nancy Fraser) was between the struggle for recognition and the struggle for redistribution. Equality was the obvious goal of the struggle for redistribution, which called for rights and material resources to be distributed more equally. But was equality even relevant to the struggle for recognition? In those struggles, what was being called for was recognition of what one *was*. That was a matter of identity. Identity has of course continued to be invoked since, under the indirect influence of Nietzsche's critique of morals and Foucault's extension of that critique to all norms and all forms of normativity, and the more it is invoked, the more uncomfortable the proponents of equality have felt in pressing their claims.

It would be a terrible distortion to say that in our time everything has changed, though change has indeed happened and some of its causes are readily identified. The financial crisis of 2008 and following, Occupy Wall Street, the Bernie Sanders campaign, the glaring difference in vulnerability to Covid-19 among different social groups, successful strikes in unlikely places like Amazon, a general reinvigoration of labor campaigns, and other recent events have all reminded us of equality's power to gather together the energies of impatience with the status quo. Of course, equality had already been throwing its weight around. Noam Chomsky has pursued a rigorously universalistic "no double standards" critique of American foreign policy for what seems like forever. Edward W. Said's challenge to American policy in the Middle East is popularly associated with his book *Orientalism* (1978) and with his identity as a Palestinian, about which he wrote with great insight, but the basis of his politics was not different from Chomsky's: equal rights for all, Palestinians and Israelis alike, in a single shared state of all its citizens. People like Stuart Hall, Adolph Reed, and Robin D. G. Kelley have been insisting for decades that there is no serious politics of race that doesn't include or place itself within a politics of class, which is to say, at least roughly, an egalitarian politics. Among feminists, Nancy Fraser has never been a lone voice crying in the wilderness, and indeed her insistence on redistribution now seems to fit snugly within a Black feminist politics of intersectionality that goes back to the 1970s and that never for a micro-second forgot economic inequality.

And, of course, matters of identity also remain very much in the forefront of politics today, and not just because of moral panics on the right about trans youth and so-called wokeness. Indigenous people have every right to demand that their children be educated in their native language. Their claim to difference can be generalized. Equality shouldn't mean sameness.

To say this is to admit that the struggle for greater equality is by no means an uncomplicated one. What does equality mean? Equality of what? Many of the champions of equality speak explicitly or implicitly in favor of equality of opportunity, not equality of resources or outcomes. To take that position is to accept the legitimacy of the competition for resources. More precisely, it is to accept competition as the proper principle by which society's resources should be allocated. In that sense, even though the loudest and most relevant critique of capitalism is that it creates such terrible inequalities, egalitarianism is not as anti-capitalist as it might seem. To demand, say, that people control the fruit of their labor is to demand something more than equality, and perhaps even something different from it.

Here is another complication. Inequalities of income, for example between men and women doing the same work, are blatant and infuriating, but they are arguably no more consequential than inequalities of total wealth, which most often depend on other factors, especially inherited wealth. More inequality comes from inheritance than from income. For many people, the largest single source of inherited wealth derives from family property. And that means that redlining, the policy by which bankers consistently denied mortgages to potential homeowners in neighborhoods where the majority was made up of people of color, has helped increase and entrench an already impressive economic inequality along racial lines.

To this I add a further complication, which I developed a few years ago in an article for the online journal *Aeon*. Are "we" really the 99%? Many of us who have applauded that stirring figure, beginning with the 2011 Occupy Wall Street movement, knew that the number was not precise and was never intended to be. The slogan did not arise because someone calculated that 99% was more accurate than 92% or 85% or 66%. It arose because it seemed to capture the grossness of a prevailing inequality. The problem is that a global perspective forces us almost to reverse the percentage. At the level of the planet as a whole, inhabitants of metropolitan capitals who proclaim "we are the 99%" are in fact much more likely to belong to the top 10%, if not to the top 1%. As many have observed, the so-called developed world accounts for a disproportionate share of the world's resources. The rich in global terms are relatively few in number, but they punch above their population weight in terms of consumption of goods and services as well as the production of toxic wastes. Internationally speaking, the official statistics on mortality rates and childhood malnourishment are similarly out of whack.

As World Bank economist Branko Milanovic has been insisting for decades, there is ample empirical evidence that the division between have and have-not countries has come to outweigh the division between haves and have-nots within any given country. Milanovic writes: "most differences in income can be attributed to someone's country of citizenship rather than their position within their own society." Thus to achieve "even simple equality within states" – already of course a utopian goal – "would make very little difference to global inequality." Inequality *within* nations, bad as it is, pales in comparison to inequality *between* nations.

Yet even those of us who find global inequality indefensible hesitate to raise the subject. Mostly because things being how they are, talking about it doesn't seem to do any immediate good, politically speaking. It sounds like moralizing in a void. The economy is supranational, while even at its best, politics seems restricted to the scale of the nation. Even where the equality of "one person, one vote" exists, and we know that this is far from the case in the United States, national citizenship does not confer any voting rights at all, let alone equal rights, on "foreigners," and this despite the fact that those foreigners are often directly affected by the policies that will be decided upon in supposedly democratic national assemblies. Since the foreigners don't vote, what political party would campaign for global economic equality? How can we even start to speak about economic equality at the global scale when the equal right to vote has no global meaning? I say all this without even beginning to speak of inequality as it pertains to refugees or, in more general terms, to precarity, another, somewhat less tangible measure of material deprivation.

Another reason for hesitation is the not unfounded fear that, if we were to take inequality with the seriousness that it deserves, to push for a more equitable distribution of existing resources (rather than miraculously managing to add new resources without furthering the extractivist model that is destroying the natural habitat), we would have to imagine sacrificing some of the comforts to which we have become accustomed. The issue is more often associated with responses to climate change, including leaving fossil fuels in the ground. Austerity not in the neoliberal sense, in which the rich get richer and rest of us tighten our belts, but in an environmental sense, which would require belt-tightening for the rich as well. Globally speaking, recall, "the rich" doesn't mean the 1%. It probably includes anyone who would be reading these words. And points at much the same political obstacle.

If we take equality seriously on a global scale, we should not imagine that afterwards we will continue to value equally those things we are in the habit of valuing, or to see them so valued by others. Certain things that have seemed to be necessities, an absolute part of who we are, will be in danger of being seen as luxuries, things we can and must learn to do without. We should not imagine that we will continue to be ourselves. We will have to become something or someone else. There are no technocratic solutions, no merely economic solutions to inequality. In that sense, equality is a program of cultural re-invention, aimed at identity itself. That does not make it any less frightening.

On this note – equality as a program of cultural re-invention – I will pivot here from the mainly material sense of equality that I have been referring to above and instead try to consider the term in a moral and cultural sense, as for example when it performs as a silent partner in phrases like "there have been atrocities on both sides." On Saturday, October 7, 2023 Hamas militants broke out of Gaza and attacked villages and army bases on the Israeli side of the fortified border, killing over one thousand noncombatants, including many women, children, and elderly people. This was an atrocity. The outrage it elicited was natural and legitimate. Equally natural and equally legitimate was the response on the Palestinian side, which reminded the world of the killing of Gazans, including women, children, and elderly people, stretching back over seventeen years, by means of Israeli bombings of densely populated areas. Given the massive support for Israel in the United States and Europe, even in the face of Israeli plans for further violence that might properly be described as genocidal – plans that have not yet been carried out as I write this, that is, still in the month of October 2023 – a sense of rough moral equality between the two sides, each with its innocent victims of violence, should perhaps count as an improvement. It would certainly be an improvement over the idea of Hamas fighters as animals and of Hamas itself as an organization that deserves to be eliminated from the face of the earth. (How easy it would be to say the same of Israel and the Israelis, who have so much more innocent blood on their hands). And yet equality of this balanced sort does not seem satisfactory.

In "The Compass of Mourning," an immediate response to the Gaza events published online at the *London Review of Books*, philosopher Judith Butler gave surprising prominence to the concept of equality. "I ask myself whether we can mourn, without qualification, for the lives lost in Tel Aviv as well as those lost in Gaza without getting bogged down in debates about relativism and equivalence. Perhaps the wider compass of mourning serves a more substantial ideal of equality, one that acknowledges the equal grievability of lives, and gives rise to an outrage that these lives should *not* have been lost, that the dead deserved more life and equal recognition for their lives." The ideal of equality referenced here sounds familiar and unthreatening. But it does not stop at "equal grievability." As Butler goes on, the ideal of equality does indeed get "more substantial." "How can we even imagine," she asks, "a future equality of the living without knowing, as the United Nations Office for the Coordination of Humanitarian Affairs has documented, that Israeli forces and settlers had killed nearly 3800 Palestinian civilians since 2008 in the West Bank and Gaza even before the current actions began. Where is the world's mourning for them? Hundreds of Palestinian children have died since Israel began its 'revenge' military actions against Hamas, and many more will die in the days and weeks to come."

As you will have noticed, Butler takes a turn here away from "equal grievability," which is to say away from "there have been atrocities on both sides." This is a turn from morals to politics. In 1676, in what white Americans of the time called King Philip's War, which drove most of the Native Americans out of New England, the Native Americans burned villages and massacred women and children, just as the settlers did. The Indians too committed atrocities. But the fact that they committed atrocities does not erase or repeal the justice of their cause. This is what I take Butler to be saying. Atrocities inspire horror. If you look them in the face, you deplore them. But true equality, like true justice, is a terminus that can only be obscured by lining up atrocities on one side against atrocities on the other. In Palestine, as in New England, the question was and is driving people off their land.

The past tense of "was" and the present tense of "is" suggest another sense in which equality is not necessarily sameness. Difference comes with time. Butler can also be understood as taking a turn that is pragmatic and temporal, as if she were saying that what we have to concentrate on *now* is not the violence that has already happened but the violence that is about to happen by way of "revenge," violence that will be committed by Israel, violence that we still might have time to do something about. From this perspective, formal equality would be deflected by time, and where we are situated in time. Violence that can still be stopped is unequal to violence that has already happened.

During the French Revolution, Edmund Burke wrote in a letter to a friend, "It is possible that many estates about you were obtained by arms, that is, by violence, . . . but it is *old violence*; and that which might be wrong in the beginning, is consecrated by time, and becomes lawful." I for one would very much like to see today's titles to land, and more generally the ways in which the rich obtained property rights over the riches that define and disgrace our very unequal society, reopened to scrutiny. Burke invites this mental experiment; he seems to want the violence that underlies so much inequality displayed for all to see. He is admitting that the results would be scandalous. And, at the same time, he is saying that the passage of time makes a moral as well as a legal difference – that old violence is not the same as new violence. I can imagine looking back at these new acts of bloody expropriation from the perspective of a future when the people of Gaza and all the other Palestinian refugees, whether from inside or outside the borders of 1948 Israel, will enjoy equal rights and protections in a state of their own choosing. The violence suffered and the violence committed will still have been terrible, but by then the violence will not look as terrible as it looks today.

Robin D. G. Kelley
Humanities in the Face of Genocide

Robin D. G. Kelley is one of the scholars I feel very fortunate to have met because of the "Humanities for Humans" project. I knew his name, his reputation, and had read some of his work prior to our online conversation, beginning, actually, with his book on the great jazzman Thelonious Monk (2009), as my husband is a huge jazz fan and reads widely on the subject. I was deeply impressed by Kelley's inspirational work Freedom Dreams: The Black Radical Imagination *(2002, 2022) for its erudition and rhetoric. I was particularly bowled over when he decided to honor the 20th anniversary reissue of that book not with emphasis on himself but by being in public conversation with creative young black scholars, activists, and artists (four sessions over 2022–23). Though we still haven't met face to face, being in a live conversation with him online was even more inspiring and a bit more intimidating than reading his books. He thinks so clearly on his feet and can move from topic to topic and citation to citation with an alacrity that is almost dizzying. He cares about what he is saying and his kind of passion for helping us understand is something I admire enormously.*

Here is what Robin D. G. Kelley shares with us about his life's journey so far.

Born in New York City in 1962, I drifted between Harlem, Seattle, Pasadena, Los Angeles, Atlanta, Ann Arbor, Greenwich Village, and back to Harlem until I settled into my current job as the Gary B. Nash Professor of U.S. History at University of California, Los Angeles. When I'm not raising kids or trying to play the piano or explaining what my middle initials stand for, I teach and write books such as, *Freedom Dreams: The Black Radical Imagination, Thelonious Monk: The Life and Times of an American Original; Africa Speaks, America Answers: Modern Jazz in Revolutionary Times; Yo' Mama's DisFunktional!: Fighting the Culture Wars in Urban America*; and *Hammer and Hoe: Alabama Communists During the Great Depression*. You can find my troublemaking essays in the *Boston Review, New York Review of Books, New York Times, The Nation, Spectre, Hammer and Hope, Dissent, Black Scholar,* and *Journal of Palestine Studies,* among others. I'm currently completing two books, *Making a Killing: Cops, Capitalism, and the War on Black Life* and *The Education of Ms. Grace Halsell: An Intimate History of the American Century*.

And here's what Robin D. G. Kelley wants to share with us in the context of this book and our times.

A poem in a difficult time
is beautiful flowers in a cemetery.

Mahmoud Darwish, "To a Young Poet"

I

When Irene Kacandes invited me to dialogue with Bruce Robbins as part of the "Humanities for Humans" series, I gladly accepted. Our charge was to discuss "systemic inequalities," what it meant, state and civil society's efforts to address inequality, and how the humanities might help us envision and create a more equal – which is to say, more just – society. We began with the word "inequality" itself, which I took to mean primarily (though not exclusively) economic inequality. The cause of economic inequality is commonly understood to be the unequal distribution of a tangible, measurable thing we call wealth. By treating inequality as a matter of creating a more equitable balance of access and ownership of the world's wealth, we evade the real source: capitalism.

Race and gender are not incidental or accidental features of the global capitalist order – they are constitutive. Capitalism seeks to maximize profits while reducing labor costs, but because it emerged as a gendered and racial regime, it extracts wealth and structures value by assigning differential value to human life and labor. In other words, capitalism operates within historically specific racial and gendered regimes that determine who is targeted for dispossession, slavery, lower wages, predatory lending, disfranchisement, and citizenship, and who has access to better schools, neighborhoods, greater home equity, and public accommodations, etc. Building on Walter Rodney's classic text, *How Europe Underdeveloped Africa*, I located the roots of modern inequality in slavery and colonialism – modes of exploitation foundational to capitalism – and linked this to Bruce Robbins's incisive reading of George Orwell's dilemma in his book, *The Beneficiary*. I cautioned against focusing on inequality between nations to the exclusion of inequality *within* nations, suggesting instead that they are inextricably linked. I argued that while wealth extracted from the colonies certainly benefited the metropoles, or what we today call the global North, not all classes within the metropoles shared the fruits of colonial exploitation equally. Surplus derived from colonies partly fueled industrial growth and *deepened* the exploitation of metropolitan workers. And, contrary to theories of a labor aristocracy, the comparative edge enjoyed by workers in the metropoles derived not from the largesse of capitalists spreading imperialist profits to the masses, but rather by organizing strong unions, often backed by socialist, communist, and labor parties emerging in the 1930s and 40s. Workers of the decolonizing nations shared these ambitions and sought to turn the colonial state into a robust welfare state to benefit working people, end poverty, provide for the social needs of all people, and protect workers' rights. Indeed, the U.S. Marshall Plan to reconstruct Europe, the creation of the North Atlantic Treaty Organization (NATO), and the litany of overt and covert interventions in Greece, Turkey, Italy, Saudi Arabia, Iran, Guyana, Guatemala, and so forth, were U.S.-led efforts to crush socialist and social democratic movements and ensure the dominance of a free market economy. Perhaps more consequential were the failed efforts by Mohandas Gandhi, W. E. B. Du Bois, and others to persuade the fledgling United Nations to declare colonialism a crime against humanity. As Du Bois lamented, to have done so would have gotten in the way of the sovereignty of the colonizing nations, and it's about preserving the Anglo-American alliance. And that's more important than the plight of 750 million people in Africa, Asia, and the Caribbean.[1]

During our original conversation, we talked about how the idea of "white privilege" masks the ways in which racism continues to exploit white workers by convincing them that they have privileges that they don't really have. We also discussed liberal discomfort and guilt generated by visualizing inequality without understanding its real source. And in both of these instances, I found in Robbins's *The Beneficiary* brilliant insights into how and why these relationships remain hidden or obscured from public view. But my chief point was that to call a process or relationship "systemic" or structural does not mean it works like a machine, producing inequality independent of human action or despite our better judgement. Rather, the system was deployed to beat back or destroy social movements challenging the power of capitalism and colonial rule. These struggles, both within the United States and around the globe, determine the shape and form of socioeconomic inequality; systemic inequality is the product of this constant give and take. The defeat of a decolonized workers' socialist or social democratic state opened the path for neoliberalism.

The conversation took place in February 2023. Irene encouraged us to expand these ideas into essays for a volume also titled *Humanities for Humans*. I'll confess, my schedule and mounting obligations made it impossible to attend to this work right away, so I set it aside and perhaps subconsciously hoped that she might forget.

---

1 W. E. B. Du Bois, *Color and Democracy: Colonies and Peace*, Harcourt, Brace and Company, 1945, 9–10.

Meanwhile, other developments in the world compelled me to think even more deeply about inequality and the role of the humanities in differentially advancing or arresting human life. Fascism had emerged as a real, existential threat. Catalyzed in part by rising inequality, fascism was also historically both a source of, and justification for, inequality. Between February and June of that year, Colin Kaepernick, Keeanga-Yamahtta Taylor, and I put together and published a book titled *Our History Has Always Been Contraband: In Defense of Black Studies* (Haymarket, 2023) in response to the right-wing attack on the Advanced Placement (AP) course in African American Studies, and the tidal wave of legislation practically criminalizing the teaching of antiracism, gender, sexuality, and anything deemed critical of the United States. "Critical Race Theory" had become a dog whistle to vilify any acknowledgment of racism, sexism, or related forms of oppression and subjugation. These laws were backed by well-funded think tanks and right-wing groups like Moms for Liberty and championed by white nationalists and neo-Nazis.[2]

Meanwhile, as I'm writing and reading and speaking and worrying about the impact of neofascism on higher education, especially ethnic and gender studies and the humanities as a whole,[3] we are learning about the escalating violence in the occupied West Bank. Settlers and Israeli Occupation Forces were killing Palestinians on a daily basis during the first half of 2023. By May, Israeli military incursions in the West Bank, most spectacularly in Jenin, took the lives of more than 130 Palestinians, displaced thousands, and forced some 250 Palestinian students to flee their universities.[4] On May 12, 2023, City University of New York School of

---

[2] Jaclyn Peiser, "N.H. governor slams conservative group's $500 reward for reporting critical race teachings: 'Wholly inappropriate,'" *Washington Post*, November 19, 2021; Wallace Hettle, "Keep History Teachers Free to Teach, in Iowa and the Nation," *History News Network* (June 20, 2021), https://historynewsnetwork.org/article/180574. In August 2022, a federal judge declared the law violates the First Amendment, the ruling does not apply to public schools or colleges, where it is still in effect. Tim Craig, "Judge blocks Florida's 'Stop Woke Act' restrictions for private companies," *Washington Post*, August 18, 2022.

[3] Much has been written on the fascist assault on liberal higher education, especially the humanities, but we too often overlook the complicity of humanities scholars in propping up fascist regimes. See Jason Stanley, "Fascism and the University," *Chronicle of Higher Education* (September 2018), https://www.chronicle.com/article/fascism-and-the-university/?sra=true; Eden McLean, "Fascism's History Offers Lessons about Today's Attacks on Education," *Scientific American* (April 7, 2023), https://www.scientificamerican.com/article/fascisms-history-offers-lessons-about-todays-attacks-on-education/.

[4] "Netanyahu's Cabinet Ministers in Race to See Who Is Most Fascist," *Haaretz* (May 28, 2023), https://www.haaretz.com/opinion/editorial/2023-05-28/ty-article-opinion/netanyahus-cabinet-ministers-in-race-to-see-who-is-most-fascist/00000188-5ef6-df79-a19d-fefe5dbb0000; Usaid Siddiqui and Federica Marsi, "Israel judicial crisis live: Parliament ratifies divisive bill," *Aljazeera* (July 24, 2023), https://www.aljazeera.com/news/liveblog/2023/7/24/israel-judicial-crisis-talks-collapse-as-parliament-votes; Jonathan Guyer, "What the siege of Jenin signals about the future of Israel and

Law graduate, Fatima Mousa Mohammed, delivered a powerful commencement address criticizing Israel's illegal occupation, apartheid policies, settlement building, and the recent wave of violent raids, criticism for which she was subjected to death and rape threats. Despite unwavering support from CUNY's Jewish Law Students Association, the CUNY Board of Trustees condemned Mohammed's address as "hate speech," and bills introduced in the state legislature and the U.S. Congress vowing to defund CUNY for alleged antisemitism garnered bipartisan support.[5]

The question of how humanities scholars should respond to fascism had begun to morph into a different but related question: what is our responsibility in the face of genocide? Indeed, *before* Israel launched its war on Gaza in retaliation for the October 7 attack, I had begun reading some of the essays in *The Betrayal of the Humanities: The University during the Third Reich*, a new book edited by Bernard M. Levinson and Robert P. Ericksen. The volume not only documents the complicity of humanities scholars in authorizing the Nazi regime (building on Max Weinreich's classic text, *Hitler's Professors: The Part of Scholarship in Germany's Crimes Against the Jewish People* [1946]), but it also addresses the initial reticence within academia to study, let alone acknowledge, the Holocaust, despite the UN's adoption of the Genocide Convention and widespread journalistic accounts of mass murder. I discovered the book not long after a new war broke out in Sudan on April 15, ostensibly between the Sudanese Armed Forces (SAF) and the paramilitary Rapid Support Forces (RSF). In reality, this conflict is a proxy war between Saudi Arabia and the United Arab Emirates, where both seek

---

Palestine," *Vox* (July 6, 2023), https://www.vox.com/world-politics/2023/7/6/23784923/israel-palestine-jenin-raid-news; Mohammed Najib, "250 Palestinian students leave their universities citing Israeli incursions in West Bank," *Arab News*, March 18, 2023, https://www.arabnews.com/node/2271081/middle-east; "Statement from Press Secretary Karine Jean-Pierre on the Visit of President Isaac Herzog of Israel," July 13, 2023, https://www.whitehouse.gov/briefing-room/statements-releases/2023/07/13/statement-from-press-secretary-karine-jean-pierre-on-the-visit-of-president-isaac-herzog-of-israel-2/.

5 Ginia Bellafante, "She Attacked Israel and the N.Y.P.D. It Made Her Law School a Target," *New York Times* (June 2, 2023), https://www.nytimes.com/2023/06/02/nyregion/cuny-law-speech-mohammed.html; "JLSA Statement in Support of Fatima," https://docs.google.com/document/d/1YuEmcjfra01kftXhi9Ui4Yb0-8v1uF9MO3asayp7rq0/edit; "H.R.3773 - Stop Anti-Semitism on College Campuses Act," https://www.congress.gov/bill/118th-congress/house-bill/3773/text Specifically, the bill uses the International Holocaust Remembrance Alliance (IHRA) definition of antisemitism, which extends to criticisms of Israeli state policies even if they violate international law, the Geneva and Hague Conventions, or the U.N. Charter and its various conventions on racism, apartheid, torture, human rights, and the like. "Human Rights and other Civil Society Groups Urge United Nations to Respect Human Rights in the Fight Against Antisemitism," *Human Rights Watch* (April 20, 2023), https://www.hrw.org/news/2023/04/04/human-rights-and-other-civil-society-groups-urge-united-nations-respect-human.

to expand their influence and power in the region and crush the popular democratic Sudanese revolution of 2018–2019.[6] Nearly all critics and scholars acknowledged that the scale of death caused by military conflict, displacement, and starvation reached genocidal proportions. That same summer of 2023, we also witnessed escalating violence in Haiti and the expansion of war in Eastern Congo, extending to Uganda and Rwanda, with China providing military support for the Democratic Republic of the Congo (DRC) to protect its own investments in cobalt mining. By most estimates, nearly 7 million people have been internally displaced by the war in Eastern Congo.[7]

Imminent threat of genocide. Humanitarian catastrophe. Such are the phrases bandied about when discussing these devastating wars over territory, resources, and power. Where are the humanities in a humanitarian crisis? Ironically, this question assumed its clearest focus for me while watching the blockbuster film *Oppenheimer* days after the anniversary of the bombing of Hiroshima and Nagasaki (August 6 and 9). There is a scene in which Robert Oppenheimer, upon witnessing the first successful detonation of the atomic bomb at Los Alamos, New Mexico, on July 16, 1945, quotes the Bhagavad Gita to no one in particular: "Now, I am become Death, the destroyer of worlds." Was this meant to be a confession? A mea culpa? A genuine fear? Oppenheimer is, after all, portrayed as the consummate humanist, a reader of Sanskrit who worships at the altar of poetry, literature, and classical music. Whatever mixed feelings he may have harbored at the moment, a few scenes later in the film, we see the learned and civilized Oppenheimer not only celebrating his fatal invention but insisting it be used on densely populated cities to demonstrate the weapon's destructive capacity. The film avoids a reckoning with the genocidal violence caused by the bombings, or the horrible effects of nuclear testing on the Indigenous communities around Los Alamos who had already suffered dispossession and now federally sanctioned poisoning. Theodor Adorno's famous line from *Negative Dialectics* came to my mind: "No universal history leads from savagery to humanitarianism, but there is one leading from the slingshot to the atom bomb."[8]

---

[6] "As war rages in Sudan, community resistance groups sustain life," Interview with Nisrin Elamin in *Don't Call Me Resilient: The Conversation* (May 30, 2024), https://theconversation.com/as-war-rages-in-sudan-community-resistance-groups-sustain-life-229885.

[7] Center for Preventative Action, "Conflict in the Democratic Republic of Congo" (May 15, 2024), https://www.cfr.org/global-conflict-tracker/conflict/violence-democratic-republic-congo#:~:text=In%20October%202023%2C%20the%20UN,three%20decades%2C%20continues%20to%20deepen.

[8] Theodor W. Adorno, *Negative Dialectics*, Routledge, 1973, 320.

II

The October 7 attack by Hamas's al-Qassam Brigades, Islamic Jihad, and other allied organizations in Southern Israel that took the lives of 695 Israeli civilians, 24 Arab-Israeli citizens (mostly Bedouin), 71 Thai and Nepalese migrant workers, and 373 police and soldiers, and Israel's disproportionate response further underscored the crisis facing humanity and the humanities. As I write these words nearly nine months into the assault, the death toll in Gaza exceeds 37,000, not counting the more than 10,000 Palestinians presumed to be under the rubble. Most of the casualties are women and children, as is the case with the more than 84,000 wounded. And with each passing day, more children die of starvation, the majority of whom are under five years old.[9] To call this a genocide, a massacre, or a war crime, or to demand an immediate and permanent ceasefire elicits accusations of antisemitism or harboring "pro-Hamas" sympathies. Labelling any criticism of Israel antisemitic has been a tried-and-true strategy of pro-Israel lobbying groups for years. However, it has so far failed to stop the largest pro-Palestine demonstrations in U.S. history. On college campuses, students have sustained an eight-month long campaign calling for a permanent ceasefire, an end to unconditional U.S. military support for Israel, divestment from companies that fuel Israel's genocidal war and occupation, full disclosure of university investments, and an acknowledgment of the loss of Palestinian life. University administrations have responded by disciplining students, suspending chapters of Students for Justice in Palestine and Jewish Voice for Peace, and calling police onto campuses to arrest students for non-violent protest.

For right-wing Republicans, some of whom are aligned with white nationalists known for their rabid antisemitism, the university had not done enough to punish the students. Under the guise of the Committee on Education and Workforce, McCarthy-like hearings charging "liberal" university presidents with allowing their institutions to become hotbeds of antisemitism have been held. If antisemitism is the primary concern, why not investigate white nationalists and Nazis whose ranks are growing? Simple. The purpose of the hearings is to fundraise for the campaigns of these politicians and to serve as a trojan horse for the right-wing attack on Diversity, Equity, and Inclusion, "critical race theory,"

---

9 "Children Keep Dying of Hunger in Gaza as Israel Continues Its Unrelenting Assault," *Democracy Now!* (June 14, 2024), https://www.democracynow.org/2024/6/14/headlines/children_keep_dying_of_hunger_in_gaza_as_israel_continues_its_unrelenting_assault.

and the university as a whole.¹⁰ These televised inquisitions forced University of Pennsylvania president Liz McGill and Harvard University president Claudine Gay to resign, and those who survived returned to their campuses and did as they were told: they ratcheted up the repression. On April 17, 2024, the day Columbia University president Nemat "Minouche" Shafik was called to Washington, D.C. to testify before the committee, students organized the first Gaza Solidarity Encampment on Columbia's campus, vowing to remain until the university divests. The very next day, after an embarrassing dressing down by Congress, president Shafik authorized the NYPD to clear the encampment and make over 100 arrests. The students reestablished their encampment the next day and sustained it for just under two weeks before president Shafik called in riot police a second time. In response, the faculty advanced a vote of no confidence.¹¹

The destruction of Columbia's encampment inspired students across the country and around the world to establish their own Palestine solidarity encampments on over 160 campuses. University administrators have been predisposed to call police to dismantle the encampments and arrest student protestors, and initiate disciplinary hearings against students resulting in suspensions, expulsions, and evictions from campus housing. Rarely have university presidents elected to negotiate or seriously consider divesting the institution's vast holdings from companies that fuel and finance the war and occupation of Palestine. The financial costs are minimal, particularly since divestment would simply entail finding new investments for existing capital. No college or university has suffered financially from divesting from apartheid South Africa, private prisons, or fossil fuel companies. On the contrary, the histories of anti-apartheid protests on campuses such as Yale, Princeton, Cornell, and UCLA are often invoked as evidence of their campus commitment to social justice. University leaders know this. Rather, they are worried about the symbolic costs of bucking what has come to be known as the "Palestine Exception." In the U.S., speech critical of Israel has been universally punished, and donors are quick to withhold gifts at the first inkling of pro-Palestine activism on campus. Calls for divestment or even a permanent ceasefire elicit absurd charges of being pro-Hamas, antisemitic, and proponents of Israel's annihilation. Trustees and donors have gone further, demanding even harsher punishments for student protesters and conspiring with the corporate

---

10 Katherine Knott, "'You Are in the Crosshairs': Higher Ed Braces for Another Antisemitism Hearing," *Inside Higher Ed* (April 16, 2024), https://www.insidehighered.com/news/government/2024/04/16/higher-ed-braces-another-round-congressional-grilling.
11 Shea Vance, "Faculty of Arts and Sciences advances vote of no confidence in Shafik as internal pressure mounts," *Columbia Spectator* (May 11, 2024), https://www.columbiaspectator.com/news/2024/05/11/faculty-of-arts-and-sciences-advances-vote-of-no-confidence-in-shafik-as-internal-pressure-mounts/.

and legal world to deny them future employment.¹² Although the latter is clearly illegal, university leaders have chosen to cower before such threats rather than stand up for the rights, well-being, and safety of their own tuition-paying students.

Scholars in all disciplines are facing severe consequences for their support of Palestine and condemnation of Israel. San Jose State Professor Sang Hea Kil was recently suspended primarily for her role as the faculty advisor to their Students for Justice in Palestine chapter. Professor Jodi Dean of Hobart and Williams College was suspended from teaching after she published an essay centering Hamas as part of a longer tradition of Palestinian resistance. Several weeks prior to October 7, Jewish activist Ralph Goldwasser, with the support of members of Congress, waged a campaign to force Princeton University to ban Jasbir K. Puar's book, *The Right to Maim: Debility, Capacity, Disability* (Duke University Press, 2017), even though Goldwasser admittedly never read the book. Puar's prize-winning study demonstrates that Israel's Occupation Forces have implemented a deliberate policy of maiming Palestinians. Goldwasser hired an LED billboard truck to circle the campus attacking Puar's book as blood libel and accusing Princeton of promoting antisemitism, alongside a large image of Albert Einstein who, by contrast, represented the good old days when Princeton was a refuge for Jews fleeing Nazi Germany.[13] The juxtaposition was striking in its elision of Princeton's own long and ignoble history of antisemitism, not to mention Einstein's own critique of the dispossession of Palestinians as the price for founding the state of Israel. In a letter dated April 10, 1948, he excoriated Jewish paramilitary groups, namely the Haganah, the Irgun, and the Stern gang for violently expelling Palestinians from their land, villages, and homes. "When a real and final catastrophe should befall us in Palestine," he opined, "the first responsible for it would be the British and the second responsible for it the Terrorist organizations [built] up from our own ranks. I am not willing to see anybody associated with those misled and criminal people."[14] Goldwasser's failed effort to have the book banned

---

[12] Prem Thakker and Akela Lacy, "In No Labels Call, Josh Gottheimer, Mike Lawler, and University Trustees Agree: FBI Should Investigate Campus Protests," *The Intercept* (May 4, 2024), https://theintercept.com/2024/05/04/josh-gottheimer-mike-lawler-campus-protests/; Paula Chakravartty and Vasuki Nesiah, "Is This the End of Academic Freedom?" *New York Times*, April 5, 2024, https://www.nytimes.com/2024/04/05/opinion/free-speech-academic-freedom.html; Ariel Zilber, "'Unforgivable': Citadel CEO Ken Griffin says he won't hire Harvard students who blamed Israel for Hamas terror," *New York Post* (October 16, 2023), https://nypost.com/2023/10/16/harvard-condemned-hamas-after-complaint-from-donor-ken-griffin/.

[13] Azad Essa, "'I didn't read it': The campaign to ban a pro-Palestine book at Princeton," *Middle East Eye* (September 24, 2023), https://www.middleeasteye.net/news/princeton-university-group-calling-for-pro-palestine-book-ban-not-read-it.

[14] Fred Jerome, ed., *Einstein on Israel and Zionism: His Provocative Ideas About the Middle East*, St. Martin's Press, 2009, 187.

proved a dangerously successful act of incitement. Puar was flooded with hate mail and death threats and all sorts of vile attacks – although this wasn't the first time.[15]

None of this is new. We can point to the firing of Professor Steven Salaita by the University of Illinois in 2015, the decision by the University of Toronto in 2020 to rescind a job offer to Law Professor Valentina Azarova for her scholarship on Palestine, the persistent attacks on Professor Rabab Abdulhadi at San Francisco State University over her work on and advocacy for Palestine, and this is only the tip of the iceberg. More than twenty years ago Palestinian scholar of British literature, Saree Makdisi, contrasted somewhat optimistically the burgeoning divestment campaign with "the entrenched, unyielding, and apparently unthinking advocates of the Israeli position on American university campuses, whose lack of intellectual integrity and moral coherence will surely cause them to become more and more isolated, their endless cries of 'demonization' and 'anti-Semitism' ringing ever more hollow with each passing day, their position proving ever more difficult to defend."[16]

Of course, the repression of U.S. scholars does not compare to what Palestinian scholars in Palestine have to endure. Oxford University Professor Karma Nabulsi coined the termed "scholasticide" to describe Israel's ongoing war on intellectuals, intellectual life, and academic institutions in Gaza, the West Bank, and East Jerusalem. Since the start of the war, every college and university in Gaza has been destroyed, and thousands of professors, administrators, schoolteachers, and students have been killed, wounded, or jailed. The case of Nadera Shalhoub-Kevorkian, a 62-year-old distinguished Palestinian scholar at the Hebrew University who studies state crimes, gender violence, surveillance, and incarceration, endured death threats and possible dismissal before being jailed overnight in a cold, filthy jail cell. Her crime? Characterizing Israel's killing of children as a genocide and calling for the abolition of Zionism.[17] But scholasticide is not new, either. Palestinian humanists have long maintained that by working within and against colonial settings, the task of interpreting culture takes place in the context of war – a war to preserve and defend cultural institutions. As the brilliant poet,

---

15 She also received death threats after the publication of her book *Terrorist Assemblages*. See Oishik Sircar, "'A Deep and Ongoing Dive into the Brutal Humanism that Undergirds Liberalism': An Interview with Jasbir K. Puar," *Humanity Journal* (January 17, 2021), https://humanityjournal.org/issue11-3/a-deep-and-ongoing-dive-into-the-brutal-humanism-that-undergirds-liberalism-an-interview-with-jasbir-k-puar/.
16 Saree Makdisi, "The Israel Divestment Campaign and the Question of Palestine in America," *South Atlantic Quarterly* 102.4 (Fall 2003), 891.
17 Damien Cave and Rawan Sheikh Ahmad, "A Palestinian Professor Spoke Out Against the Gaza War. Israel Detained Her," *New York Times* (June 12, 2024), https://www.nytimes.com/2024/06/12/world/middleeast/palestinian-professor-israel-gaza-war.html.

playwright and activist Samah Sabawi argued, Israel has systematically dismantled Palestinians' commercial, cultural, and artistic infrastructure since its inception. Prior to 1948, Palestine boasted of dozens of bookstores, 161 newspapers and magazines, the second highest high school enrollment in the Arab world, and a massive body of literature in Arabic held in private hands and libraries. What wasn't destroyed during the Nakba ended up in the collections of Israel's National Library. Palestinians are barred from reclaiming these rare texts on the basis of absentee property laws that render all of this stolen property "abandoned."[18] The theft, closure, and destruction of Palestinian libraries and archives extended to the occupied West Bank, Gaza, and East Jerusalem following the 1967 War. Once again, Palestinian libraries and archives were seized and placed in repositories in West Jerusalem largely inaccessible to scholars in the Occupied Territories. Israel not only took possession of stolen books but banned the importation, distribution, and circulation of many books on Palestine or Palestinian issues, including literature and poetry. The Israeli occupation forces also closed the Arab Studies Society for four years, confiscated its books and documents, and damaged the library and its archives.[19] Since October 7, the Israeli military has completely or partially destroyed scores of bookstores, museums, and libraries in Gaza, including the Edward Said Library in Beit Lahia, Gaza's only English language library. Ironically, this library was founded by poet Mosab Abu Toha from books he pulled from the rubble after Israel's 51-day war on Gaza in 2014. Its librarian, Doaa Al-Masri, was among the casualties of this war. She was killed, along with her parents and siblings and countless librarians and archivists.[20]

---

18 Samah Sabawi, "A comprehensive analysis of the arguments surrounding the call for a cultural boycott of Israel," *Tales of a City by the Sea* [blogpost] (December 18, 2012), https://talesofacitybythesea.com/2012/12/18/a-comprehensive-analysis-of-the-arguments-surrounding-the-call-for-a-cultural-boycott-of-israel/.
19 Rachel Mattson, "Libraries Under Occupation: A Conversation with Palestinian Librarians," *Progressive Librarian* (Winter 2017), 113–127; Gish Amit, "Salvage or Plunder? Israel's 'Collection' of Private Palestinian Libraries in West Jerusalem," *Journal of Palestine Studies* 40.4 (Summer 2011), 6–23; Hannah Mermelstein, "Overdue Books: Returning Palestine's 'Abandoned Property' of 1948," *Jerusalem Quarterly* 47 (Autumn 2011), 46–64.
20 Dan Sheehan, "Israel Has Damaged or Destroyed at least 13 Libraries in Gaza," *LitHub Daily* (February 6, 2024), https://lithub.com/israel-has-damaged-or-destroyed-at-least-13-libraries-in-gaza/; Israeli Damage to Archives, Libraries, and Museums in Gaza, October 2023 – January 2024: A Preliminary Report from Librarians and Archivists with Palestine, https://librarianswithpalestine.org/gaza-report-2024/.

III

On May 16, 2024, two weeks after UCLA's Chancellor Gene Block ordered the police to clear our Palestine Solidarity Encampment and arrest student campers who had just endured two days of violent attacks from Zionist and neo-Nazi mobs, Howard Gilman, the Chancellor of the University of California, Irvine, called in riot police to clear that university's encampment. My friend and colleague, UCI Global Studies Professor Tiffany Willoughby-Herard was arrested while she tried to protect her students. Her arrest and "perp walk" through campus was caught on video as local media attempted to interview her. She managed to give a minute-long masterclass on the complicity of the university with imperial violence – at home and abroad – the immiseration and precarity created by gendered racial capitalism, and the university as a contested terrain. "We cannot have a genocidal foreign policy in a democracy," she cried. "These young people are going to be the ones that have to pay the price for these horrible decisions. These police officers out here today, that's thousands of students' scholarships. Thousands of students that could have been able to go to school and have books and have housing. But instead, our Chancellor, who is a very cruel man, decided to send thousands of dollars' worth of state funding paid for by the taxpayers into the trash." When asked if she was concerned about jeopardizing her job, she replied in a single sentence that still brings tears to my eyes: "What job do I have if the students don't have a future?"[21]

In sixty seconds, while being zip tied and dragged away by riot police, Professor Willoughby-Heard put in bold relief the questions facing humanities scholars – indeed all scholars and intellectuals – in the twenty-first century. What is our responsibility in the face of fascism and genocide? How do we refuse and resist complicity when our own institutions are becoming or have become complicit? How do we contribute to creating a just world where poverty, precarity, patriarchy, capitalism, racism, homo- and transphobia, ableism, fascism, and genocide are unthinkable? Does the university as a space to nurture free, independent, radical thinking have a future? The current mass uprising for a free Palestine, especially the student encampments, have created a genuine crisis for the university. The demand for a critical, engaged humanities for humans has never been more urgent, more consequential, as we face both a rising tide of fascism and an ongoing genocide. The choice before us is complacency – i.e., complicity – within the

---

[21] The video was reposted thousands of times on a variety of platforms. See, for example, Margaret Kimberly @freedomrideblog, https://x.com/freedomrideblog/status/1791144520970543275. Accessed May 25, 2024.

neoliberal university, or refusal and resistance. The latter are what brought us Black Studies, Ethnic Studies, Women and Gender Studies, Queer Studies, Disability Studies, and other epistemic challenges that have fundamentally altered the humanities – at least in some circles. We must remember how we got here – like every other movement for liberation and justice, by protest, occupation, rebellion, and deep study. In other words, we might follow the lead of the Palestine solidarity encampments.

Rebecca Tsosie
Indigenous Sustainability and an Ethic of Place: Can We Protect the Lands that We Love?

Rebecca Tsosie is another scholar I was fortunate to meet because of this project. My dear colleague at Dartmouth, N. Bruce Duthu, put me in touch with her when I asked him about Indigenous scholars particularly interested in environmental issues. I was fascinated by Tsosie's combination of specializations: law, philosophy, and Indigenous studies. She brings each to bear on the subject at hand in an enlightening way. I appreciated her willingness to prepare for our session on "Imagining Anew the Future of the Earth," and appreciated the way she and Harriet Hawkins easily discovered commonalities. When I had the opportunity to meet her in person during a visit of mine to Tucson, Arizona where she teaches a few months after our "Humanities for Humans" session, I not only enjoyed our conversation but also delighted in watching the students who were walking by and their eagerness to greet her. It was obvious how much they admired her. Her responses were graceful and professional. She exudes a wisdom that I and obviously they love being in the presence of.

Here's Rebecca Tsosie's biographical sketch about herself.

I started my academic career when I attended UCLA as an undergraduate student and undertook to complete the newly minted M.A. degree in American Indian Studies as part of an Interdisciplinary Humanities Bachelor's Degree. I had grown up in Los Angeles near an urban Indian Center. I knew very little about my own people (Yaqui), but the elders at the Indian Center encouraged all of us to learn more about our communities and attend local Native cultural events, such as pow-wows. I attended UCLA after completing a summer bridge program, and I learned so much about Native American history, culture, and religion. I loved reading the literature of Native writers and poets, including Simon Ortiz, Leslie Marmon Silko, Louise Erdrich, and N. Scott Momaday. I had the most wonderful faculty members, including Dr. Duane Champagne (Turtle Mountain Chippewa/ Sociology), Dr. Jennie Joe (Navajo/Anthropology), Professor Carole Goldberg (Law), and Professor Kenneth Lincoln (English). I was fascinated by the work of Professor Vine Deloria, Jr., who wrote so eloquently and from an Indigenous perspective about law and policy, philosophy, and theology. I took Federal Indian law at the UCLA law school as an undergraduate student, and I became so angry when I read the nineteenth-century cases and many of the twentieth-century cases. For the first time, I understood how the past shapes the current day, and I became passionate about achieving justice for Native people. At the encouragement of Carole Goldberg, I applied for law school and was admitted to the J.D. program at UCLA. I also completed a President's Postdoctoral Fellowship after graduation and worked for a law firm in Phoenix.

I started my teaching career at Arizona State University, and I was the first faculty Executive Director of ASU's Indian Legal Program and served in that position for fifteen years. I also held an academic appointment with the faculty of Philosophy within the School of Historical, Philosophical, and Religious Studies and served as an affiliate faculty member for the American Indian Studies Program and a Distinguished Sustainability Scientist for the Global Institute of Sustainability. In 2016, I joined the University of Arizona law faculty. I am currently a Regents Professor and Morris K. Udall Professor of Law at the James E. Rogers College of Law at the University of Arizona. I teach Federal Indian Law, Property, Constitutional Law, Cultural Resources Law, Jurisprudence, and Critical Race Theory. I work on issues of diversity and inclusion in higher education and have served as Vice Provost for ASU and for the University of Arizona in an effort to foster those values.

I am a legal scholar, but my work is interdisciplinary and strongly rooted in the humanities. I work on environmental and cultural resources issues, and I also work extensively on human rights law and the articulation of Indigenous sovereignty and self-determination. I am dedicated to fostering justice for Native communities, and I have worked on a pro bono basis for tribal court systems. I also do pro bono work for tribal communities on cultural resources issues, as well as health and education issues. I am a member of the Arizona Bar Association and the California Bar Association.

I love teaching and have been honored to mentor many students who have become influential leaders for Native people. I consider my legal education to be a great blessing because it enables me to help those who are in need. My educational path challenged me to question the traditional disciplinary approaches and to interrogate injustice. I continue to advocate for transformation in the law.

In addition to the work on environmental sustainability and climate justice cited in the chapter I'm contributing to this volume, my recent writings include the following: "*Accountability for the Harms of Indigenous Boarding Schools: The Challenge of Healing Persistent Wounds of Historical Injustice*," (Southwestern Law Review, 2023); *Justice as Healing: Native Nations and Reconciliation* (ASU Law Journal 2023); *Tribal Data Governance and informational Privacy: Constructing Indigenous Data Sovereignty* (Montana Law Review, 2019); "*Constitutional Law and Epistemic Injustice: Hate*

Speech, Stereotyping, and Recognition Harm," a chapter in Paul Giladi and Nicola McMillan, *Epistemic Injustice and the Philosophy of Recognition* (Routledge Press, 2023).

Here is Rebecca Tsosie's reflection on how Indigenous attitudes of stewardship can help us all.

Introduction

I recently attended a Tribal environmental conference held upon the beautiful lands of the Viejas Band of Kumeyaay Indians in San Diego County, California, where I gave a keynote lecture on the conference theme: "This Land that We Love." The Kumeyaay people, like many Indigenous Nations, have a longstanding commitment to the land, water, and air that is built upon respect for the natural systems that have enabled our survival, generation after generation. Former Chairman of the Pyramid Lake Paiute Tribe, Mervin Wright, gave the conference's opening remarks, and he spoke from his cultural knowledge about the core elements that all humans and animals need to sustain life: the land (earth); the fire (sun, lightning); the water (rivers, clouds); and the air (wind). These elements combine in a generative process that creates food and energy, but this process also requires human knowledge and care. Other conference participants affirmed this truth in the context of their traditional Indigenous farming and harvesting practices, as well as traditional forest management practices, such as "cultural burns."

An ethic of stewardship orders tribal environmental planning, standing in sharp contrast to the dominant view of U.S. society that land, water, food and energy are "commodities," and that "natural resources" serve human needs. To have "love for the land" is much different, and it embodies a distinctive type of thinking that unites many Indigenous peoples, across different places and cultures. The primary difference is that Indigenous peoples belong to their traditional lands and territories in a way that unites the present generation with past generations and secures the place of the future generations. Oren Lyons, a Faithkeeper for the Haudenosaunee people, describes this ethic as "thinking for the seventh generation," and there are corresponding beliefs among many Indigenous peoples throughout the world, who collectively comprise many distinct cultures and religions.[1] Thinking ahead for the benefit of the "seventh generation" represents an ethic of sustainability that emphasizes permanence, stability, and balance.

---

[1] See Rebecca Tsosie, "Indigenous Sustainability and Resilience to Climate Extremes: Traditional Knowledge and the Systems of Survival," 51 Connecticut L. Rev. 1009, 1013 (2019).

The concept of "Indigenous sustainability" embodies a place-based notion of the relationship of a people to a particular set of lands and waters. In that sense, for Indigenous peoples, "sustainability" is the result of conscious and intentional strategies designed to secure a balance between human beings and the natural world, and to preserve that balance for the future generations. This also means that human beings have a responsibility to the land and water. The framework of "responsibility" is very different from the framework of "rights," although today we need both frames to govern effectively.

In comparison, U.S. law and policy tend to differentiate each "resource" and manage it separately: land, water, energy, food, forests, fish, and wildlife. Tribal, state, and federal governments each have a share of management authority, but many resources are managed to maximize their economic value and therefore private ownership is also important.

When I gave a lecture in Hawaii a few years back, I learned of the concept of "Aloha Aina," which is deeply held by the Native Hawaiian people and translates to "love of the land." I learned that Aloha Aina has always been a central idea within Native Hawaiian thought, cosmology, and culture. According to Professor Jon Osorio, Director of Native Hawaiian Studies: "Aloha Aina is a relationship not just with land but really with nature itself and, in particular, that part of land and sea and streams and water that actually sustains life." In this sense, the land "feeds" all living things and "everything is directly dependent and interdependent with the aina."[2]

The concept of "aloha aina" combines an ecological, spiritual, and cultural understanding of the relationship between land and people. The spiritual dimension is unique to Indigenous peoples because they have been part of specific places for centuries. In that sense, Queen Liliukalani described the Native Hawaiian people as "children of the soil" and distinguished them from the political citizens of the Kingdom of Hawaii prior to its overthrow, which included a handful of non-Native people who were residing in Hawaii. The non-Native people were colonists who "owned" sugar cane plantations, and they were the ones who conspired to overthrow the Hawaiian Monarchy and work toward annexation. Today, the "Kingdom of Hawaii" is invisible to the tourists who flock to the state of Hawaii.

The U.S. Supreme Court has failed to recognize the political rights of Native Hawaiian people on a similar basis to the status held by federally recognized tribes. Today, in other words, Native Hawaiian people lack the same political sovereignty as tribal governments. All citizens of Hawaii can buy and sell the land, and they manage (or mismanage) the water. Tourism brings thousands of people to the Ha-

---

2 See Steele, Julia. Episode 2: The meaning of aloha aina with Professor Jon Osorio, www.hawaiipublicradio.org.

waiian Islands each year. They all share responsibility for the mass pollution and contamination that is destroying the fragile marine resources of Hawaii. Under an Indigenous view, the non-Native people are visitors (guests) on the land. The Indigenous people are the "children of the land" with the duties and responsibilities to land, water, fish, streams, volcanoes, and every other aspect of the natural world. The catastrophic Maui fires that occurred in August 2023, devastating the community of Lahaina, brought this dichotomy into sharp focus. In the nineteenth century, Lahaina was the capital of the Kingdom of Hawaii and embodied a beautiful and sacred landscape that had been stewarded for generations. After Hawaii was annexed into the United States, the lands were developed into a resort playground for wealthy tourists. The causes of the 2023 fire are still contested, but it is clear that those in power did not appreciate the sacred nature of the lands, nor did they protect that fragile and vulnerable landscape in a time of climate change. As a result, over 100 people perished, 1200 homes and buildings were destroyed, and over 11,000 residents were displaced.[3] Not surprisingly, the land speculators rushed in, extending offers to "buy" properties from homeowners who still owed mortgage payments for underinsured homes that were fully or partially destroyed and would take years to rebuild.[4] The Lahaina community, drawing upon its love for the Aina, formed a "land trust" to rehabilitate the community, but it is unclear whether they can raise the necessary funds to enable the community to stay in place and rebuild.

The only way to truly protect the land is to adhere to the place-based values that are associated with Indigenous concepts of "sustainability."[5] Indigenous sustainability fosters environmental protection, but most people do not understand the connection. Today, Indigenous peoples comprise less than 5% of the world's population and occupy 25% of the earth's surface, but those lands also house 80% of the world's biodiversity.[6] Perhaps more people could appreciate the values of Indigenous sustainability if they knew this fact.

Writing here mainly as a legal scholar, I will discuss what "love of the land" could mean within the context of the Law.

---

3 Nina Lakhani, "First came the Maui wildfires. Now come the land grabs: 'Who owns the land is key to Lahaina's future," *The Guardian*, Friday, March 15, 2024.
4 Lakhani, "First came the Maui wildfires."
5 Rebecca Tsosie, "Rethinking Reconciliation: Land-Based Citizenship and Indigenous Futures" (forthcoming chapter in a volume on Environmental Citizenship).
6 See Mike Ludwig, "UN Report Says Indigenous Sovereignty Could Save the Planet," *Truthout* (May 7, 2019) (summarizing content of the 2019 United Nations Climate Assessment, documenting the status of the earth's terrestrial systems).

The law of the land and rivers

Although I teach Federal Indian law at the University of Arizona, I always start my class by telling the students that the most important set of laws for Native people comes from Native Nations themselves. Tribal codes are similar to state codes in terms of the written laws that govern civil and criminal cases, as well as regulatory issues, such as hunting and fishing permits. But there are also customary laws that Indigenous Nations have had for generations and that still govern the relationship between the people and the land, as well as other human beings and "other-than-human" people. These "traditional laws" may not be written down, and the knowledge of the law may reside with cultural and spiritual leaders.

Tribal customary law is often quite ancient and might be associated with an "original" law that existed at the time of creation and orders the natural world.[7] Some Indigenous Nations, such as the Dine, call this the "fundamental law" because *it doesn't change*, and because there is a moral duty that accompanies human interaction with the environment. In that sense, this type of "traditional law" represents scientific knowledge of the environment over generations ("TEK"), but it also has a built-in system of environmental ethics to regulate human conduct. Within this relational world, humans have duties and responsibilities. They should not treat land, water, and food as "commodities." Rather, these sacred aspects of the natural world enable our collective survival.

In some Indigenous traditions, aspects of the natural world have "personhood," and there are duties of care and respect that are owned by human stewards. For example, the White Earth Ojibwe community has created a law to protect "Mnoomin," which is the personification of Wild Rice. The Maori people successfully obtained legal "personhood" for a river that is of great cultural and environmental significance. Wild salmon are considered "other than human" persons for many Indigenous peoples in Alaska and the Pacific Northwest.

Of course, traditional law is largely invisible to external entities, such as state, local and federal governments. Federal Indian law regulates the relationship between federally recognized tribal governments and the U.S. government under a "trust" model. The United States, as trustee, holds legal title to trust land on the reservation, but the "beneficial" title is in the Tribe, and, therefore, land, water, forests, fish, and other species on the reservation are considered to be "tribal trust resources." The Trust model maintains that the federal and tribal governments should cooperatively manage these resources, and the Environmental Protection Agency over-

---

7 See Rebecca Tsosie, "Indigenous Sustainability and Resilience to Climate Extremes," supra note 1 at 1017.

sees many programs that are part of this model. The trust model is an important form of governance, but it is incomplete, when compared to traditional law.

Traditional law describes the ancestral territory that the Native people "belong to." The Territory of the Kumeyaay people, for example, extended across what is now the U.S./Mexico border, and it clearly comprised a larger area than the trust land of the tribal government's current reservation, inclusive of regional rivers, streams, wetlands, pasture area, and forests. What role does the Kumeyaay nation have in governing their ancestral territory that now exists outside of the reservation?

The answer to that question exists within international human rights law. The Declaration on the Rights of Indigenous People (2007) states that Indigenous peoples have the right to self-determination, which is a moral and political right to "autonomy" that belongs to all "peoples." It was not until 2007 that there was a consensus that Indigenous peoples are "peoples" with a right to self-determination, including the right to govern themselves upon their ancestral territories. Under domestic Federal Indian law principles, tribal law generally extends to tribal members and tribal trust lands within the reservation, but it often does not extend to non-Native conduct that takes place outside the reservation. There are other political barriers that are caused by contemporary international and state borders. Increasingly, we must consider collaborative governance to effectively protect the lands and waters of the Territory.

It has never been more important for tribal governments to work cooperatively with the federal and state governments to protect their ancestral territories and waters. And in that respect, I would highlight the language of the UN Declaration on the Rights of Indigenous Peoples, Art. 25, which states that:

> Indigenous peoples have the right to maintain and strengthen their distinctive spiritual relationship with their traditionally owned or otherwise occupied and used lands, territories, waters and coastal seas, and other resources and to uphold their responsibilities to future generations in this regard.

That language should form the orienting framework to involve Native Nations in collaborative management of territory, inclusive of rivers, ocean, and forests, across borders and jurisdictional lines.

The human rights construct of "self-determination" validates the claims of Indigenous peoples to be included within environmental decision-making that impacts their traditional territories.[8] The inclusion of Indigenous peoples serves the

---

[8] See Rebecca Tsosie, "Indigenous Peoples and Environmental Justice: The Impact of Climate Change," 78 U. Colo. L. Rev. 1625, 1654–1657 (2007).

unique cultural interests that Indigenous peoples have in relationship to their traditional lands and waters. It is also a corrective for the actions of nation-states that appropriated Indigenous lands and removed Indigenous peoples from their territories. Today, there is a powerful social justice argument to reconcile these past wrongs and their continuing consequences. Finally, it can be argued that the right of Indigenous peoples to cultural survival is jeopardized by destruction of their traditional lands and waters. This is true, for example, for the Cocopah people in Mexico, who are the "People of the River" and built a beautiful life on the Colorado River delta before the dams shut down their access to the river and polluted the smaller streams in their territory. The U.S./Mexico border split the Cocopah people. The Cocopah tribal government on the U.S. side has a reservation, a successful economy, and legally protected water rights. The Cocopah people in Mexico lost their livelihood and relationship with their river, and they cannot continue their cultural way of life. That human rights violation should be rectified in the ongoing adjudication of the Colorado River. Unfortunately, the rights of the Cocopah people in Mexico have been largely invisible in the negotiations.

The changing structure of power: Federal/state/tribal

The political sovereignty of federally recognized tribal governments is framed by what the United States Supreme Court has described as the status of a "domestic, dependent nation." This means that federally recognized tribal governments retain sovereignty over their reservation trust lands and their members, but they are subject to the Supremacy of the United States and the "Plenary Power" of Congress to enact laws in its role as trustee. This model of tribal sovereignty is the predominant mode of Indigenous self-determination in the United States.

Congress, acting as "trustee," can do many things to assist Native Nations, but it can also do things that are quite harmful, such as unilaterally abrogating treaty rights, or taking tribal land or water in exchange for money. The United States can even "terminate" a tribe's "trust" status and suspend or terminate the privileges that would otherwise apply to the group. The logic of the Trust model is that the federal government protects tribal rights, and therefore, it excludes state power. This exclusive political relationship is embedded in the Commerce Clause, which gives Congress the sole and exclusive authority to regulate commerce with Indian tribes (as well as with foreign nations and among the several states).

The U.S. Supreme Court has upheld the longstanding principle that tribal governments have "inherent sovereignty," but it has also held that Congress has the power to terminate the powers associated with sovereignty to "complete defeasance." That is why some members of the Supreme Court currently challenge whether tribal governments really do have "inherent" sovereignty in the sense of international governments. Are they "political" groups or "racial" groups? That question was presented to the Supreme Court in summer 2023, and the Court upheld the Indian Child Welfare Act as a permissible exercise of Congressional authority, but it did not decide the "equal protection" issue regarding whether Indian children can be treated "differently" for purposes of state adoption proceedings.[9] The *Brackeen* case illustrates why it is so important for tribal governments to have their own laws and judicial institutions as they exercise the active power of tribal sovereignty.

The federal/tribal relationship is undergoing revision by the current Supreme Court, causing questions to arise about state power and its impact on tribal land, water, and people. I will focus on a recent case, the Supreme Court's reading of the trust responsibility in the context of tribal reserved water rights. In *Arizona v. Navajo Nation* (which was consolidated with *DOI v. Navajo Nation*), the U.S. Supreme Court held that the Navajo Nation could not state its equitable claim for breach of trust against the United States on the basis that the U.S. had failed to protect or secure the Nation's reserved water rights in the Colorado River.[10] The rights have not yet been quantified and there is no decree or settlement of Navajo water rights in Arizona. The 9th Circuit held that the Navajo Nation had stated an equitable claim for breach of trust because the Nation has an 1868 Treaty reservation with significant federal reserved water rights (Winters rights), which is a trust resource. Even though the Navajo Nation does not have a final decree quantifying their rights, they at least have an equitable claim that their trust resources should be accounted for and protected, as the U.S. and its agencies manage the Colorado River in a time of drought. This case is important because half of the 22 tribal governments with reserved water rights in Arizona have *not* yet achieved a final settlement or decree.

In an opinion authored by Justice Kavanaugh, a majority of the Court applied the very stringent standard that is used to assess whether a tribe can sue the United States for damages in the Court of Claims for breach of fiduciary duty. The Court reasoned that the Tribe was alleging that the U.S. had a duty to enable access to water, which could only happen with costly infrastructure. The Court held that there is no trust duty in the federal government to take affirmative steps to secure water for a tribe. The Court stated that the U.S. has no duty to develop

---

9 Haaland v. Brackeen, 143 S.Ct. 1609 (2023).
10 Arizona v. Navajo Nation, 599 U.S. 555 (2023).

tribal land and therefore no duty to develop tribal water. If the Tribe had a final decree and if someone was interfering with the tribe's access to water, the U.S. role as trustee would kick in. Otherwise, tribal "water rights" are inchoate and of no legal effect.

What is the remedy? The Court stated that even though the U.S. government had blocked the Navajo Nation's effort to intervene in the Colorado River litigation at the most critical juncture in the history of that legal proceeding (between 1960 and 2000), the tribe *currently* has a right to intervene, and therefore the Navajo Nation is not "harmed" because it can "protect" its own rights in court.

Justice Gorsuch wrote a dissenting opinion (joined by Kagan, Sotomayor, and Jackson) in which he argued that there was no doubt that the U.S. government is holding treaty lands and reserved water in trust for the Navajo Nation, and therefore, there is no barrier to an equitable action asking the U.S. to do an accounting to identify the water rights it is holding for them. Because the U.S. alone can "manage" these waters – the tribe cannot do so independently – and because the U.S. blocked the earlier motion to intervene in the court proceeding, the U.S. is now held to an equitable duty to identify the reserved rights set aside by treaty.

The majority in the Navajo Nation case argues that the U.S. is a sovereign, and it cannot have any "fiduciary" duties unless it expressly creates them and says it will be bound. It did not do so in the 1868 Treaty, although it assumed other duties (such as providing seeds and farming implements for three years). The dissenting justices alone upheld the trust doctrine as it has been structured under Federal Indian law for generations, including the canons of construction, the "bare" or limited trust that can be enforced through declaratory or injunctive relief, and the "full fiduciary duty" which is enforceable in damages if breached. At the time that the trust "resource" no longer exists, the cause of action for damages is all that is left. However, where the trust resource still exists, the U.S. should have a duty to protect and conserve the resource on behalf of the tribe, and that is the basis for an "equitable" cause of action.

Of course, the respective arguments about the trust responsibility are in some ways a distraction from the original wrong. The Colorado River was originally allocated pursuant to a 1922 Compact among seven Western states. Tribal governments were not invited to participate, and they were referred to only loosely as being under "federal" protection. Although all parties were aware that the tribes had reserved water rights, their rights were largely invisible because they were not quantified at that time. Today, tribal governments are significant rights holders. In Arizona, tribal water rights to the Colorado River comprise at least 40% of Arizona's allocation, and nearly 30% of the land within Arizona is actually tribal land.

"Love of the land," inclusive of associated waters, is a key part of Arizona's future, and we must reconstruct our systems of governance to recognize this fact.

Indigenous governance and Indigenous futures

With respect to collaborative governance of shared resources that transcend jurisdictional lines, it is more helpful to think of tribal inherent sovereignty according to its cultural frame. In an article that I co-authored years ago with Wallace Coffey, a colleague on the Native American Rights Fund Board and Chairman of the Comanche Nation, we identified "cultural sovereignty" as "the effort of Indian nations and Indian people to exercise their own norms and values in structuring their collective futures."[11] The Native Hawaiian people also have cultural sovereignty, even though the U.S. government is not giving full effect to their political sovereignty.

Inherent sovereignty is the "heart and soul" of the Native community, upon its land, and over time. Inherent sovereignty does not come "from" the U.S. government, and therefore the U.S. cannot "destroy" tribal sovereignty, although it can ignore or disclaim the interest. If Native people do not relinquish their sovereignty, it is retained, whether or not external governments recognize this. The Supreme Court regularly changes the contours of tribal "political" sovereignty to serve the interests of the United States or the state governments. However, "cultural sovereignty" is completely within the control of Native communities, and it is what has enabled Indigenous peoples to survive several centuries of colonization.

Cultural sovereignty is expressed when Indigenous communities fight to protect sacred places on federal "public lands," such as Oak Flat, a sacred site to the Apache people in Arizona. In 2014, Congress authorized an appropriations bill that carried a rider providing for the transfer of U.S. Forest Service land at Oak Flat to the Resolution Copper Company for use as a copper mine. The land transfer has been challenged on many grounds and it is not yet final.[12] If the proposed land transfer goes through, Oak Flat will transition from federal ownership (which carries some duty to consult with tribal people and attempt to mitigate harm) to private ownership. Tribal political sovereignty is not effective over non-Indians on private fee land, unless there is some distinctive reason to consider tribal interests (such as the need to protect ancestral remains that are excavated when lands are developed).

---

11 Wallace Coffey and Rebecca Tsosie, "Rethinking the Tribal Sovereignty Doctrine: Cultural Sovereignty and the Collective Future of Indian Nations," *12 Stanford Law and Policy Review* 191, 196 (2001).
12 Most recently, a majority of the 9th Circuit Court of Appeals, sitting en banc, ruled against Apache Stronghold, an organization representing the interests of Apache people to continue practicing their religion and culture at the sacred site, and affirmed an earlier District Court opinion and 9th Circuit decision allowing the transfer to move forward. Apache Stronghold v. United States, 954 F.4th 608 (9th Cir. En banc, 2024).

Cultural sovereignty entails a process of repatriation: of tribal wisdom, land, and cultural heritage. The important dynamic is for external governments – whether state or federal – to give effect to the human right of Native people to self-determination.

The right to self-determination can be expressed through the Trust/sovereignty model, but it is also a basis for asserting rights to collaborative governance of "public lands" such as the model established when the Bears Ears National Monument was created in 2016. Collaborative management is necessary for the effective governance of shared resources, such as water and forests, that extend across jurisdictional boundaries. The Colorado River basin is a prime example because it is shared by seven states, thirty tribal governments, and Mexico, requiring an ethic of collaboration.

What does the future hold?

We are in a time of "climate crisis," which I will define here as escalating levels of greenhouse gas emissions that cause higher temperatures and related changes, such as melting of the glaciers and sea level rise. The impact of severe storms, floods, and drought has hit every continent. There is an international conversation about the "right" of developing countries to continue to develop their fossil fuel resources, as well as the economic "rights" of multinational corporations to extract energy resources. These "economic development" arguments are often positioned as "justice" for underdeveloped countries. However, the severe and increasing planetary impacts should caution against relying on the "rights" framework.

At the international level, "sustainability" is generally linked to the concept of "sustainable development," which should meet the needs of the present generation without compromising the ability of future generations to meet their own needs. The concept of intergenerational equity was originally part of the sustainability calculus, but it became subsumed within the conversation about "climate equity," which recognized that developed nations had contributed the most to the problem of climate change and therefore should bear the economic burden passed by curtailing greenhouse gas emissions so as to allow the countries of the global South to develop their resources. The United States rejected the idea of "common but differentiated responsibility," and politicians argued that if China and India could escalate fossil fuel development, this excused the obligation of the United States to issue binding emissions limits on greenhouse gas emissions. We have been stuck in this conversation for decades.

The notion of social justice for the global South resonated with adherents of the environmental justice movement in the United States, who noted that the burdens of environmental contamination fell heavily upon poor and minority communities, who were often promised jobs in the mining or industrial sectors. Wealthy and predominantly White communities escaped the burdens of pollution because their high land values and restrictive zoning laws screened out most harmful industries. This conversation is still occurring in the United States as companies attempt to reach settlements around contamination of land and drinking water by the so-called "forever" chemicals, such as PFAS. This limited tort model is not useful in the context of harms for "climate justice," because there are multiple causal factors, as well as catastrophic intergenerational impacts upon species and the world's land and water systems.

The future requires us to reconcile human rights with earth rights. If we see those two sets of rights as being in opposition, we get the result that we have today. In the context of the Colorado River, the river is vastly overused and cannot sustain itself under the current structure. Litigation over "water rights" is costly and takes decades. We don't have that kind of time, and there is no way that one party can "win" and one can "lose." We will all lose if the Colorado River cannot survive.

Conclusion

The ethic of "love for the land" is consistent with an ethic of healing and regeneration. By coming together, we can make a commitment to the well-being of human communities and the environment. That is the framework we need for a healthy and resilient future.

Imagination has a central role in addressing the problem of climate change. As Valerie Brown observes in the context of her work on "wicked problems," the decision-maker of the future has an obligation to go beyond standard ways of thinking that might emerge from a single avenue of inquiry and be open to different ways of thinking.[13]

Embedded within Indigenous law are ancient systems of knowledge that represent the best scientific understanding of "place" over time, as well as a land ethic that fosters permanence, stability, and resilience. President Biden has instructed federal agencies to work with Indigenous communities to integrate Indigenous knowledge into federal decision-making. His administration re-

---

13 See Valerie A. Brown, John A. Harris, Jacqueline Russell, *Tackling Wicked Problems Through the Transdisciplinary Imagination*, Routledge, 2010.

leased policy guidance recognizing that "to make the best scientific and policy decisions possible, the Federal government should value and, as appropriate, respectfully include Indigenous knowledge."[14]

Climate resilience describes the capacity of a community to restore itself and thrive, even after a negative event. Most Indigenous peoples have been remarkably resilient over the past centuries, and they possess very strong adaptive systems. However, because the current challenges are multiple and involve social and economic impacts, it is very likely that many Indigenous peoples will once again face involuntary relocation due to coastal erosion, drought, flooding, and storm damage. In fact, Indigenous communities in the Arctic are currently at "ground zero" for climate impacts.

Whereas Indigenous peoples understand their responsibility to natural systems, they are caught in the language of "rights" for purposes of Western law. Sheila Watt-Cloutier, an Inuit leader and human rights advocate, asserted that climate change is jeopardizing Inuit culture and traditional lifeways. She brought a human rights petition in the Inter-American Commission on Human Rights, seeking to force the United States to curtail greenhouse gas emissions. Although the petition was later dismissed on procedural grounds, the language used by the Inuit people is instructive about the future:

> what we are doing here is we are defending our right to culture, our right to lands traditionally used and occupied, our right to health, our right to physical security, our right to our own means of subsistence, and our rights to residence and movement. And as our culture is based on the cold, the ice and snow, we are in essence defending our right to be cold.[15]

The Inuit people are masterful at adapting to a harsh climate that seems unliveable to many. They have much to teach external societies, but they are increasingly vulnerable in a fragile world where ice and snow behave differently than ever before, where polar bears drown in the winter, and salmon die in hot summer waters. The experience of the Inuit people is not visible to many people who live in distant cities, consuming food purchased from well-stocked grocery stores, and living and working in buildings where the temperatures are moderated by

---

14 See Memorandum for Heads of Federal Departments and Agencies, dated November 30, 2022 and entitled "Guidance for Federal Departments and Agencies on Indigenous Knowledge." (Executive Office of the President).

15 Sheila Watt-Cloutier, "The Inuit Right to Culture Based on Ice and Snow," *Moral Ground: Ethical Action for a Planet in Peril*, eds. Kathleen Dean Moore and Michael P. Nelson, Trinity University Press, 2010, 23–29, here 28.

heating and air-conditioning units. In those artificial environments, climate change is often dismissed or overlooked in the order of everyday priorities. We cannot afford that level of delusion as we step into the future we have created. Engaging Indigenous peoples in the places that they steward is a necessary first step to reshaping climate governance.

Part Three: **Crafting Connection**

Harriet Hawkins
All Power to the Imagination

I was not very familiar with the academic study of Geography until I arrived at Dartmouth College. What I discovered, at least in the Dartmouth department, was a huge variety of methodologies and disciplines where the scholars practicing them still seemed to have a common language that allowed them to share on many different topics. Some of those topics overlapped with my interests, and I quickly became friends with several "geographers." It was two of these geographer friends who happily supplied me with the name of Harriet Hawkins when I asked about geographers who might be interested in talking about climate change in a Humanities context. They characterized Harriet as a dynamo, a whirlwind, brilliant, and perfect for the topic, and so I experienced her as well. I was thrilled that she was involved in something called "GeoHumanities"! I was also very pleased for our series that Harriet would be bringing examples from her experiences in many different places on planet Earth as well as from her home context of Britain. (I have asked the publishers to retain British spellings and punctuation below to signal that perspective.) I strongly recommend checking out her website where I saw for the very first time a warm invitation to anyone who shares research interests to "please get in touch!"

Here's what Harriet Hawkins herself shares about those interests.

As an undergraduate I was lucky enough to stumble across the links between the interests of Geography as a discipline – in space, place, and environment – with those of artists, art historians, and theorists. In my work since then I have been interested in the geographies of art works and art worlds. Without wanting to "reduce" art works to having to "do" something, I am interested in understanding what art might "do in the world", how it "makes worlds", including more environmentally sustainable and socially just worlds. In exploring these ideas, I am interested in overarching concepts such as creativity, imagination, and aesthetics, as well as in innovative methods, asking for example, how researchers might not only study existing art works, but also collaborate on the production of new works. I have been lucky enough to work with a range of wonderful academics and artists, and arts organisations around the world, to explore their art works and exhibitions and ask questions of their effects, but also to create spaces and infrastructures to enable the production of new art works and exhibitions. In order to support these goals, in 2016 I co-founded the Centre for the GeoHumanities at Royal Holloway University of London, to help support ongoing conversations between geographers interested in questions of space, place, and environment, and arts and humanities scholars and practitioners interested in the same concerns. Aside from organising events, editing journals, and collaborating on art works and exhibitions, I write. My books include *Creative Geographies, Making Worlds* (2012); *Creativity: Live, Work, Create* (2016); and *Geography, Art, Research* (2020). I am currently working with a group of artists and academics on projects exploring creative approaches to the pasts, presents, and futures of the subsurface, exploring caves, underground infrastructure, geologic forces, and Indigenous cosmologies, in the United Kingdom, Italy, Cambodia, Mongolia, the United States, Norway, Iceland, and Singapore.

And here's what Harriet would like to share with us about the imagination, a topic that we've seen is important to all our contributors.

Imagine the Earth in 500 years' time, or even in 5000 years' time. What comes into your head? What about 10,000 years into the past?

Did you imagine a future of environmental catastrophe, with billionaires living in luxury in bunkers and many millions more living as climate refugees? Or did we manage to halt climate change, regreen the world, and alleviate ever-deepening inequalities? Is your imagination shaped by the vivid worlds penned by your favourite Sci-Fi writer – utopian or dystopian – or is your imagination shaped by a Christian world-view of new creation? Potentially, I wager, it is some mix of these and likely many more.

What about your imagination of the past? 10,000 years ago the Earth was just emerging from the freezing grip of the Ice Age, and agriculture as we know it was beginning to take place. How far back can you imagine before you lose a grip on the way the world might have been?

Even such simplistic imaginative exercises offer a lens onto how we, as individuals and as societies, frame our worlds, and pace and space our lives. Yet it is easy to overlook, or even to dismiss, the formative power of the imagination; it is just something in our heads, a flight of fancy, a nice escape with little purchase on the material world. If this is your imagination of imagination, you might be surprised to find that the imagination has come to the fore of late in discussions of environmental crisis. In the West at least, we are used to registering environmental crisis and its solutions in terms of science and technology, their successes and failures. Yet, it has become increasingly common for environmental commentators of our day to point to the environmental crisis as a crisis of the imagination. This line of thinking implicates our imaginations as both a cause of environmental concerns and as a site of their possible solutions. This is quite a claim, one that I will explore further in what follows, considering what it means to explore the environmental crisis as a crisis of the imagination, and how such understandings might direct us to action and solutions.

A crisis of the imagination?

In the opening days of 2023, activist and writer Rebecca Solnit penned a think piece for the UK edition of the Guardian newspaper.[1] It was headlined "if you win the popular imagination, you change the game, why we need new stories on climate." It was part of the promotion for her new edited collection with Thelma Young Lutunatabua, *Not Too Late, Changing the Climate Story from Despair to Possibility*. During the course of her discussion, Solnit expands on her ideas of popular imagination as follows:

> every crisis is in part a storytelling crisis. This is as true of climate chaos as of anything else. We are hemmed in by stories that prevent us from seeing, or believing in, or acting on possibilities for change. Some are habits of mind, some are industry propaganda. Sometimes, the situation has changed, but the stories haven't, and people follow the old versions, like outdated maps, into dead ends.[2]

As a geographer, I am drawn to this cartographic metaphor and its suggestion of imaginations as mappings of life. Imaginations here emerge less as private escapes from the material realities of the world, and more as integral to the individual and collective pacing and spacing of lives. Solnit and Young Lutunatabua's take on the climate crisis as an imaginative crisis foregrounds the possibilities of stories as a particular mode of the imagination. If, as they contend, we currently have the wrong stories – of despair, of apocalypse, and of relations to the world that lead to inaction – we might look for more stories of existing hopeful presents and of "liveable futures". These stories, they argue, might enable us to shape the popular imagination away from despair to possibility, and, in so doing, resource new imaginations of the world. In their call to the imagination, Solnit and Young Lutunatabua reprise an often made connection between imagination and social

---

[1] Rebecca Solnit, "The Long Read: Why we need new stories on climate," January 12, 2023, *The Guardian*, https://www.theguardian.com/news/2023/jan/12/rebecca-solnit-climate-crisis-popular-imagination-why-we-need-new-stories.
[2] Rebecca Solnit and Thelma Young Lutunatabua, *Not Too Late: Changing the Climate Story from Despair to Possibility*, Haymarket Books, 2023.

change: figuring imagination as the first step in change, and by so doing, as the slogan goes, "making other worlds possible". First you imagine the world you want, then you bring it about, or to borrow a phrase from the 1960s radical avant-garde: "all power to the imagination!"

Solnit is by no means the first to link environmental crisis and the imagination. In 2016 Amitav Ghosh observed the cultural aversion artists and writers had to portraying the environmental concerns as "The Great Derangement". Climate crisis is, he writes, "a crisis of culture and thus of imagination". He reflects further:

> are the currents of global warming too wild to be navigated in the accustomed barques of narration? But the truth, as is now widely acknowledged, is that we have entered a time when the wild has become the norm: if certain literary forms are unable to negotiate these torrents, then they will have failed – and their failures will have to be counted as an aspect of the broader imaginative and cultural failure that lies at the heart of the climate crisis.[3]

Tracking this formulation of environmental crisis and imaginative failure leads us to the work of humanities scholar Lawrence Buell, who, writing ten years earlier in 1996 of that great nineteenth-century American environmental story-teller Thoreau, observed, "with our environmental crisis comes a crisis of the imagination. We need," he continues, "to find new ways to understand nature and humanity's relation to it."[4]

These imaginative crisis are often understood as predicated on the "modern" separation of nature and culture – a separation which foregrounds relations based on distance and difference, thus enabling violence and damage. In the place of this separation, desirable imaginations are based in attunement and entanglement, understood to precipitate relations of empathy and care. While not talking specifically about the imagination, philosopher Claire Colebrook suggests that the necessary shift in Western human-environmental relations is akin to the reckoning brought on by Darwin's Theory of Evolution.[5] No small challenge then.

In the eight years or so since Ghosh diagnosed The Great Derangement, there has been an intensified outpouring of responses which have seized these imaginative challenges and sought those "new ways" Buell called for. We can, I am sure, all bring to mind our own memorable examples of the evolving genre of climate fiction and cinema or renewed forms of eco-art. We see, too, the growth of arts organisations whose remit is to shape our cultural responses to climate and

---

[3] Amitav Ghosh, *The Great Derangement: Climate Change and the Unthinkable*, Chicago University Press, 2016.
[4] Lawrence Buell, *The Environmental Imagination, Thoreau, Nature Writing, and the Formation of American Culture*, Harvard University Press, 1995.
[5] Claire Colebrook, *Death of the Post-Human: Essays on Extinction*, Volume One, Open Humanities Press, 2014.

wider change, including groups like Cape Farewell, whose tagline runs, "Climate is Culture – where creativity shapes our ecological future."[6]

What is more, academics from across the environmental and geohumanities have produced a range of studies of the space-times of Western environmental imaginations and the challenges they pose to understanding, thereby taking action in the face of environmental crisis. Literary scholar Rob Nixon, for example, explores what he calls the "Slow Violence" of environmental destruction, the "slow and long-lasting calamities" that "patiently dispense their destruction", while some of us are diverted by more spectacular forms of environmental harm. How, he asks, do we plot and give shape in our narrative forms and representational choices to "formless threats whose fatal repercussions are distributed across space and time?"[7] What kinds of creative forms might be up to the imaginative task of slow violence? We might ask too, what kinds of creative practices are up to the task of these distributed geographies of environmental change. We might think of art works that, for example, enable audiences in art galleries in European and North American cities to listen in on melting glaciers or on changing sonic environments of islands vanishing under rising seas.[8]

Importantly, it is not just in arts and humanities that we find links between environmental crisis and the imagination, but in science and the wider academy too. Indeed, the crises in the imaginations of scientists, and other academics working on the environment, are seen as myriad. Scientists have been accused of a poverty of imagination, of being caught up in existing thinking, of being unable to think boldly or differently enough. Scientists, the argument goes, need to imagine better. In an echo of Ghosh's cultural aversion, it is claimed that scientists too have an aversion to imagining the significance of environmental crisis, and that they for a long time failed to speak stridently enough, often cowed into moderation by political forces. Again, the solution is new imaginations, the imagination of new "intellectual climates" to release us from an experimental myopia restricting our thinking around possible action and solutions.[9] In a paper for the journal *Nature Climate Change*, twenty-two critical environmental social scientists and humanities scholars asked:

---

6 https://www.capefarewell.com.
7 Rob Nixon, *Slow Violence and the Environmentalism of the Poor*, Harvard University Press, 2011, 10.
8 H. Hawkins and A. Kanngieser, "Artful climate change communication: overcoming abstractions, insensibilities, and distances," *WIREs Clim Change*, 8 (2017), https://doi.org/10.1002/wcc.472. See for example https://www.oceanicrefractions.org.
9 Noel Castree, William M. Adams, John Barry, et al., "Changing the intellectual climate," *Nature Climate Change* 4 (2014), 763–768. https://doi.org/10.1038/nclimate2339.

what would global change research look like if the critical social sciences and the wider humanities were central to its "integrated" and "actionable" intellectual ambitions? What would the modus operandi of environmental change science and technology be if everything from cultural anthropology to eco-art was an equal partner in designing projects and disseminating research outputs?

Here then is an imagination of working beyond disciplines, of drawing together different forms of knowledge as equal partners. Stunting the development of this imagination of new knowledge coalitions that work both beyond disciplinary silos and beyond the so-called ivory tower, is another imaginative problem – one that has been termed the "crisis imagination". This denotes the sense in which the imagination of the scale and urgency of environmental problems is actually limiting action, suspending robust debate and foreclosing the time and space needed for the depth of thought required by the issues. To be caught up in this crisis imagination is to be caught in a mindset that limits us from really thinking otherwise, from imagining all the possibilities for change. In short, the imagination and its failures are not just issues for scholars to diagnose in relation to environmental crisis, but importantly there is an imaginative crisis at the heart of the ways the academy has traditionally produced knowledge about the environment.

There is, then, a lot at stake in questions of imagination and the environment, and whether or not the imagination can save us. What's at stake runs the gambit from Solnit's concern with the need to shape popular imaginations – we just need better stories – to Ghosh's call to recognise our cultural aversion to imagining crisis, to Buell's desire to reimagine the relations of some humans with their environments. Important too are calls across the academy to develop nothing short of new imaginations of knowledge that will be up to the task of forging new Earth Futures. The stakes of these claims leave those of us in the arts and humanities with a number of responsibilities. We need not only to study these existing imaginations and the crisis they might be in themselves, or to participate within, but also to potentially aid in the production of new imaginations, which might alleviate these crises. Further, we might also need to press in a little harder to these ideas of the imagination, to interrogate our imaginations of imagination if you will. For if the problem is imaginations in crisis, and if, as some have posited, imaginations might save us, then to address these imaginative failures it might help to understand the imagination itself a little further, leading me to my next set of reflections.

Imagining imagination?

What comes to mind if I ask you to imagine the imagination?

Is it something a bit indulgent, perhaps the figure of the daydreamer floating free from reality? Or, perhaps the imagination for you is something almost evil, a distraction, a sleight of hand diverting us from real issues?

On Tuesday 28th May 1751 an essay on "the hazards of definitions" appeared in the *Rambler*, a two-penny sheet, sold twice weekly in London.[10] In its opening paragraphs Samuel Johnson, literary titan of the era, presented the imagination as the apotheosis of a critical object that would, in his terms, embarrass the definer:

> Imagination, a licentious and vagrant faculty, unsusceptible of limitations and impatient of restraint, has always endeavored to baffle the logician, to perplex the confines of distinction, and burst the enclosures of regularity.[11]

Johnson sits in a long lineage of those who have identified one of the more fundamental crises of the imagination – that of definition. To Johnson's vision of imagination as impatient, baffling, perplexing and bursting, we might add, twentieth-century philosopher Ed Casey's reflection of imagination as mocking the thinker.[12] The root of such mockery lies in imagination's multiple and contradictory understandings. Is it to be diminished, to be understood as mesmeric? As Casey writes, responses over the years have ranged

> from distrust to disgust, from malevolence to meconnaissance. Whilst, at the opposite end of the spectrum, for Edgar Alan Poe, the imagination was the Queen of the Facilities, for Baudelaire, the creator of the world. Even within two most common imaginations of imagination, imagination diminished, and imagination as mesmerising, we find imagination's vagrancy and mockery at work.[13]

It is the association with the fictive and illusionary that is often the driver of those who diminish imagination's power and force. Afterall, the argument goes: imagination won't save us, it is all in our heads, frivolous fun, flights of fancy, escapism with no real-world purchase. Such diminishments have their roots in the ideological communities that shape modern Western culture's desire to sort human experiences into the real and the unreal, and, which separate the material

---
10 Available from: https://quod.lib.umich.edu/cgi/t/text/text-idx?cc=ecco;c=ecco;idno=004772607.0001.004;view=text;rgn=div2;node=004772607.0001.004:11.2.
11 Samuel Johnson, *Rambler*, no. 125, May 28, 1751.
12 Edward Casey, *Imagining: A Phenomenological Study*, Indiana University Press, 2000.
13 Casey, *Imagining*, 10.

faculties of a body, passionately involved in the world, from the dispassionate reasoning of an immaterial, rational mind. For many commentators, it was during the European Enlightenment that the imagination really ended up in the doghouse of knowledge – less however due to its diminishment, than through what Lorraine Daston has memorably termed, science's "fear and loathing of the imagination."[14] Indeed, she notes that until around 1830 there was no real opposition of the imagination to science. This changed as both objectivity and the idea of scientific fact hardened, and as imagination was loosed from being understood as subservient to will and reason. Imagination's subservience was seen as vital for its proper harnessing, without which it could become dangerous. As long as art and science shared a common goal of truth to nature, they also shared a code of aesthetic, epistemological, and moral values. Yet, as art became more interested in mystical originality and quasi-divine inspiration, concerns with truth to nature slipped away, a more darkling, wild form of the imagination emerged. As the practices of science solidified, hearts hardened further to the imagination, shifting from a sense of fear to one of loathing. As Daston explains, driving imagination's loathing in this era was its so-called "orgy of overestimation" by Western Romantic artists, writers, and intellectuals. For the Romantics, the imagination was mesmerising, with a virtually limitless power. It was situated as the resolving force for many of the confrontational ideas that had come to shape thought. It offered the chance to reconcile humans with nature, the subjective with the objective, matter with spirit, the finite with the infinite, the conscious with the unconscious. It enabled relations to be formed between the static and the dynamic, the passive and the active, the ideal to the real, the universal and the particular. So powerful was the imagination that James Engell could observe, seldom "has one idea in Western Culture excited so many leading minds for such a stretch of time. It became an impelling force in artistic and intellectual life, in literature and philosophy, even in much political and social thought."[15] It is perhaps not a surprise that we continue to feel the effects of the Romantic idea of the imagination today. For some, this manifests in the enduring divisions between science and art, and in the division of artistic practice from mimetic representation. For others, it offers the foundational idea that secular art could fabricate new world views, including evolving new relations between humans and nature. The promise and burden of these expectations continues today. Indeed, we can trace the

---

14 Lorraine Daston, "Fear and Loathing of the Imagination in Science," *Daedalus* 127.1 (1998), 73–95. http://www.jstor.org/stable/20027477.
15 James Engell, *The Creative Imagination. Enlightenment to Romanticism*, Harvard University Press, 1981.

inheritances of the mesmeric imagination to the faith Solnit and others put in the imagination, and to their disappointment at its failures.

How though should we today respond, especially in the context of climate change? Should we adopt a measured tone, shake our heads and assert imagination's limits, reprising its diminishment, or even its fear and loathing – after all, the environment crisis is a serious business, and certainly the imagination can't save us. Or, should we embrace imagination's optimism, joy and possibilities, and risk, by so doing, getting carried away in a neo-romantic orgy of imagination's overestimation?

Imagination – what next?

It seems to me that the imagination still has currency, since so many of the struggles of our time are being articulated as imagination battles. Writer and activist adrienne maree brown, for example, observes how entrenched racist imaginations render some bodies and lives as less liveable. She writes, "I often feel I am trapped inside someone else's imagination, and I must engage my own imagination in order to break free."[16] Brown directs us importantly to a tension at the heart of the imagination – it is both that which can set us free, but also that which does violence. We might think, too, of the work of humanities scholars such as Edward Said, Thongchai Winichakul, and Benedict Anderson, whose concepts of Orientalism, the Geo-Body and Imagined Communities, respectively, that for all their differences, all explicitly direct us to the force of the imagination and its profound role in shaping lived worlds.[17] Crucially though, they remind us of the always present "other" to imagination's generative possibilities. That is, with evolving new imaginations comes the need to navigate existing ones, the violence they do, and the ways some imaginations might tether some people while enabling others.

What does this mean for the role of imagination, if any, in saving us? Humanities scholar Lauren Berlant manages to balance the sense that imaginations might both offer many possibilities, while also posing many challenges, including involving significant labours in its mobilization.[18] In their important trilogy on national senti-

---

16 adrienne maree brown, *Emergent Strategy: Shaping Change, Changing Worlds,* AK Press, 2017.
17 Edward Said, *Orientalism,* Penguin, 1978; Thongchai Winichakul, *Siam Mapped: A History of the Geo-body of a Nation,* University of Hawaii Press, 1994; Benedict Anderson, *Imagined Communities: Reflections on the Origin and Spread of Nationalism,* Verso, 1983.
18 See, for example, Lauren Berlant, *Cruel Optimism,* Duke University Press, 2011.

ment, a number of imaginations can be identified, but the one that emerges perhaps most memorably is the American Dream of the Good Life. Berlant's account of what they call the cruel optimism of the Good Life skewers it as something many millions continue to aspire to – a stable job, a home, car, kids, holidays – even while the pursuit of this once achievable norm is damaging in its ever-receding possibility. Of course, for many it was never a possibility to begin with. Even as Berlant diagnoses the cruelty – the attritional nature – of ongoing optimistic attachments to such good life imaginations, there are, they note, still possibilities for flourishing; there are people and organisations committed to trying to imagine and bring about other futures. Reflecting on imagination and change, they observe

> you have to imagine the world that you could promise, the world that could be seductive, the world you could induce people to want to leap into. But leaps are awkward, they're not actually that beautiful. When you land, you're probably going to fall, or hurt your ankle or hit someone.[19]

Imagination, then, for all its possibilities, is work, a leap into an unknown, a tough, often tension-filled challenge. To embrace the generative potential of the imagination is to appreciate that just as imaginations might inspire, enable, and intensify life for some, they might also erode, diminish, and silence others. It is to appreciate that for those doing the leaping this is not easy; that escaping the tethers of existing imaginations might be harder than it first seems, and that the landings – the new imaginations so expectantly desired – might not be generous and giving. These observations of imagination's labours are perhaps less about tempering our imaginative capacities or restricting desires, but instead serve as a call to pause in our rush towards imaginations as our saviour. If we want to believe in imagination's power – and I do – then we need to reflect on how, who and what is at stake as we seek to loosen the holds of existing imaginations and as we try to draw others into collective projects of imagining the world and our relations to it and to each other anew.

---

[19] Lauren Berlant in "No one is Sovereign in Love: A conversation between Lauren Berlant and Michael Hardt," December 5, 2011, published 2019 online at: http://coalition.org.mk/archives/646?lang=en, last accessed October 6, 2023.

Liz Lerman and Martha Minow

Turning Controversy into Connection

Edited Transcript from February 21, 2024 Conversation

Next, we have a transcript of the actual conversation that took place orally. It has been lightly edited for coherence and clarification. As a conversation, it had three participants, the two experts and me.

As mentioned in an earlier section of the book, I did not know Liz Lerman's work before Martha Minow suggested her to me as a conversation partner for Minow. When I did explore it, I was truly embarrassed that I had not known of her before because of the breadth and profundity of topics she's engaged, and I was even more embarrassed when two of my closest friends in the dance world immediately responded very enthusiastically to my sharing that Lerman would be speaking in the "Humanities for Humans" series. Once contact was actually made for our preparation discussion, I was struck most by two things: Liz Lerman's affection and respect for Martha Minow, and Liz's simply stated but clearly profound wisdom about human nature. This sense of her wisdom was reinforced when I worked closely with the transcript of the original conversation for the purpose of its publication here.

Here's what Liz Lerman wants to tell us about herself.

From a piece about my days as a go-go dancer in 1974 to an investigation of origins that included putting dancers in the tunnels of the Large Hadron Collider at CERN[1], I have spent the past four decades trying to make my artistic research personal, funny, intellectually vivid, and up to the minute. A key aspect of this work is opening my process to various publics, from shipbuilders to physicists, construction workers to ballerinas, resulting in both research and outcomes that are participatory, relevant, urgent, and usable by others.

Born in Los Angeles and raised in Milwaukee, I attended Bennington College and Brandeis University, received my B.A. in dance from the University of Maryland,

---

[1] Editor's note: CERN is the acronym for Conseil Européen pour la Recherche Nucléaire [European Council for Nuclear Research], a research center located near Geneva, partly in Switzerland and partly in France.

and an M.A. in dance from George Washington University. In 1976, I founded Liz Lerman Dance Exchange and cultivated the company's unique multi-generational ensemble into a leading force in contemporary dance until 2011, when I handed artistic leadership of the company over to the next generation of Dance Exchange artists.

New projects and partnerships have since emerged. I have conducted residencies on creative research, the intersection of art and science, narrative in dance performance, and the Critical Response Process, a facilitated method that I developed in 1990 for guiding feedback on creative works in progress. Hosts of me and my projects have included Harvard University, Yale School of Drama, Wesleyan University, Guildhall School of Music and Drama, and the National Theatre Studio among many others.

My performance piece, *Healing Wars*, toured across the United States until 2015, and my most recent piece, *Wicked Bodies*, premiered in April 2022. I have published several books including *Teaching Dance to Senior Adults*, *Hiking the Horizontal*, *Critical Response Process*, and *Critique is Creative* (the last two titles were co-authored with John Borstel). I have conducted Critical Response Process (CRP) workshops internationally, and 2024 marks the sixth year of the Critical Response Process Certification Program, a 10-month mentoring and peer-to-peer study and practice intensive.

With gratitude, I have been the recipient of several honors, including the 2023 Guggenheim Fellowship, 2002 MacArthur "Genius Grant" Fellowship, 2011 United States Artists Ford Fellowship in Dance, and the 2017 Jacob's Pillow Dance Award. My work has been commissioned by the Harvard Law School, the Lincoln Center, the American Dance Festival, the Kennedy Center, and others. During my senior fellowship with Yerba Buena Center for the Arts, Brett Cook and I showcased a retrospective, *Brett Cook & Liz Lerman: Reflection & Action*, from October 2022 until June 2023.

Current projects include building the *Atlas of Creative Tools*, an online resource, and *Legacy Unboxed*, a series of research performance events called *My Body is a Library*. A new collection of essays will also be published by Wesleyan University Press in 2024. I am an Institute Professor at ASU's Herberger Institute for Design and the Arts and a fellow at the Center for the Study of Race and Democracy. Married to storyteller Jon Spelman, we have a daughter, documentary filmmaker Anna Spelman.

Martha Minow has been a hero of mine since I first read her work in spring of 1995. I remember the circumstances and the article very clearly: I was participating in an interdisciplinary seminar on "Cultural Memory" at Dartmouth College organized by my colleagues historian Leo Spitzer and Shakespeare scholar Jonathan Crewe, and as a group we read and discussed Minow's 1993 article "Surviving Victim Talk" (UCLA Law Review). I felt like Minow's diagnosis of U.S. America's love affair with victimhood was very accurate then, and alas, it still is today. When I put together the very first proposal for a talk series and when I was given the green light to start organizing it, Martha Minow was in the front of my mind. I was absolutely thrilled when she agreed to speak, and the only challenge for me was figuring out which of the many topics she had thought and written about so trenchantly would be the best for a "Humanities for Humans" conversation. Martha herself immediately suggested Liz Lerman as a profound and brilliant artist, commentator, and interlocutor, and though, as I mentioned above, I was at the time unaware of Liz's prodigious talents, I was quickly convinced that this was the right pair and the right topic. In the long process that organizing such conversations and now this volume inevitably is, Martha was immediately responsive to all my emails – for which I was and remain enormously grateful, since it is not always the case among academics in general and especially not among those who are in high demand as she is. As just one small example, when I asked the group of contributors to this volume to produce a biographical sketch in the first person, Martha sent hers that same day.

And here it is.

I pursued graduate work in education and in law with hopes of participating in civil rights and human rights advocacy in the face of exclusions and injustices in the world. I have had the good fortune to find in the legal academy the ability to reflect on deeper and broader questions underlying problems such as unequal schools, conflicts between ethnic and religious groups, racialized economic and social opportunities. Drawing on history, psychology, philosophy, and empirical research, my own research addresses human rights issues affecting members of racial and religious minorities, children, persons with disabilities, and gender-linked discrimination. With the freedom to "own my own mind," and not be bound to the interests of a particular client, I have been fortunate to pursue questions about the predicates of a constitutional democracy, the risks to public accountability arising when governments rely on private contractors, the scope of acceptable force within military action, and what contributes to and what could mitigate ethnic and religious conflicts. Group-based unfairness and restrictions on individual liberty are notably at risk with the rise of digital communication and the rise of "artificial intelligence," so my recent work has turned to social media regulation and AI governance.

My books include *Saving the News: Why the Constitution Calls for Government Action to Preserve the Freedom of Speech* (2021); *When Should Law Forgive?* (2019); *In Brown's Wake: Legacies of America's Constitutional Landmark* (2010); *Partners, Not Rivals: Privatization and the Public Good* (2002); and *Between Vengeance and Forgiveness: Facing History After Genocide and Mass Violence* (1998). Recent publications include "The Unraveling: What *Dobbs* May Mean for Contraception, Liberty, and Constitutionalism," in Lee C. Bollinger and Geoffrey Stone, eds., *Roe* v. *Dobbs: The Past, Present, and Future of a Constitutional Right to Abortion* (2024); "Equality, Equity, and Algorithms: Learning from Justice Abella," 73 U. Toronto L.J. 163 (2023); "Distrust of Artificial Intelligence: Sources and Responses from Computer Science and Law," with Cynthia Dwork, *Daedalus* (2022), https://www.amacad.org/sites/default/files/publication/downloads/Daedalus_Sp22_22_Dwork-%26-Minow.pdf, and "Social Media, Distrust, and Regulation," with Newton Minow, Nell Minow, and Mary Minow, in Lee. C. Bolling and Geoffrey R. Stone, eds., *Social Media, Freedom of Speech, and the Future of Our Democracy* (2022).

Litigation, legislation, social programs, and political advocacy efforts have afforded chances to test ideas and learn: about access to justice through service on the Legal Services Corporation (a federally-created nonprofit funding civil legal services centers across the country) and work as co-chair of the Access to Justice project of the American Academy of Arts and Sciences; about international human rights, on the Countering Violent Extremism through the Center for Strategic and International Studies Commission, the board of the Iranian Human Rights Documentation Center, and advisor to the U.N. High Commissioner for Refugees; about disability rights through the Center for Applied Special Technology partnership with the federal Department of Education; with Public Counsel, about seeking judicial remedies for unequal education. I also have learned much from board service in public media (WGBH) and private media (CBS), and in philanthropic support of social change efforts. As a professor of law for more than 40 years, I have also had the opportunity to serve as dean of Harvard Law School and to teach across Harvard University and collaborate with people from other disciplines and with generations of students.

Here's the promised extract from our conversation. I point out that it begins in medias res because the opening of the conversation is already available as part of the De Gruyter blog series. With regard to edits here, I removed some distracting signs of oral delivery like "fillers" and "back-channeling" remarks, as well as a touch of repetition and some restarts. Liz Lerman added to this version more about her eight miracles for Hannukah, as that was a bit too truncated in the original oral conversation to follow easily. Otherwise, this is what we said to each other and the audience that day, which I remind readers of these lines was February 21, 2024.

Liz Lerman

Critical Response Process (CRP) is a formal process for giving and receiving feedback. As you come to understand the process, its values become clearer, and in time, you can move around in it and not just follow the sequence. In fact, you can use it in a multiplicity of ways, although most people come upon it as a four-step process and use it in that format. In dance, you practice the steps, but dancing is not just about the steps; it's about much more than that. It's the same with the Critical Response Process. We practice these steps because it's a way to learn the steps and help you practice values that are hard to keep in the urgency of our lives. There are many variations and many applications.

Here's how it works. Someone presents something, a work in progress. It can be artwork of some kind but also a plan, a brochure, or a curriculum. Anything that you want to get feedback on. As listener, the first step is to let people know that what they just did was meaningful. This could be something interesting, provocative, surprising, delightful. It can be a small detail such as, "I noticed the way this sentence sets up the rest of the paragraph." This is not to be confused with giving compliments. In our culture, we dismiss a compliment as not being genuine. We ask in this first step that people offer something in a spirit of good will. And we, in that first step, are not to bring up the things that are problematic. I'm not saying that you have to forget that something was problematic. It's just that you don't lead with it. And truthfully, if you have a really good conversation about things, it's possible that your own opinion might change as the process proceeds.

In the second step, the person who's made the work asks questions about their own work of those who have seen it. This can be hard for makers because often our issues in our work don't appear as questions, but rather as doubts or even insomnia. I like to say: dignify your apologies and worries by turning them into inquiry. The people responding to these questions have a different filter than in the first step. Now they can answer positively or negatively, but they cannot change the subject. I believe that when a person asks a question, they are saying something like "I am open to hearing whatever you have to say about this topic." It doesn't mean that they are open to hearing anything you have to say. Sometimes we say, answer what was asked, not what you wish they had asked. The responder can respond with a negative thought, but they can't change the subject.

For example, if I say to you, "How do you like the ending of my dance?" you can tell me that you don't like it, but you can't say the ending of my dance is fine, but I don't like your hair. I didn't give you permission to talk about my hair. This is where things so often go off the rails. For instance, if my daughter invites me into her room to give her help with her homework, fine. But she hasn't given me permission to tell her to clean up her room. That wasn't the contract. That wasn't the invitation. We all know what happens next: they slam the door, and, by the way, the result is no homework and no clean room! So, you have to be listening. You said that right away, Martha, when we first started talking today. The first thing you brought up in this conversation was listening.

In the third step, responders get to ask their question. Here, the challenge is to try to make the questions neutral, to stay curious, to gather information. By neutral, we mean try not to embed your opinion or assumption in the question. There are a lot of reasons to attempt this. One is, it allows the responders to consider their own reactions and to see if they are correct for this exact moment in time. Another reason to avoid embedding your opinion in the question is that non-neutral questions will usually make the person getting the feedback go on the defensive. Once defensiveness starts, it is difficult for discovery and learning to continue.

In the final step, there is a little ritual. The Responder can say something like, "I have an opinion about. . ." and they name the category, and then also add, ". . . would you like to hear it?" And the person receiving the feedback can say yes or no. This is consent driven.

In summary:
1) There are statements of meaning from the responders to the artist or the maker;
2) The artist asks their questions;
3) The responders ask their questions; and
4) Opinions are given with permission only. That's the process!

Irene

I think some of us are familiar with some of this, but having it put together for us in a sequence is very helpful. So, I'm going to up the ante, so to speak, and comment that I can see how that sequence works well with the child and the homework and even with creative work and getting feedback. But what happens with a situation like Israel-Palestine – to take this to one of the most extreme cases of controversy or disagreement in today's world? Martha, you've done so much work in international relations. Can I ask you: how do we take these principles that make so much sense when we think about them in our everyday lives and try to apply them to these situations that seem insoluble or are being "resolved" by terrible physical violence and destruction?

Martha

Let me say first that, I don't have answers, but I have questions. One question is: who's the "we" in that question and in that relationship? Ultimately, one hopes there will be some kind of a diplomatic solution. We hope that someday – we don't know when, not whether it's this year or 10 years from now – there will be an end to violent conflicts, to killing each other.

Here's another question: who's going to pursue responses to intractable conflicts? Who's going to be willing to do that?

I don't know the exact identity, but at some point, it's going to be human beings!

We'll have to sit down together and figure out a modus vivendi. How do we live together? I do know some people who are starting to talk about that. However, most of the political leaders who are relevant are not talking.

I think there's another way, and it concerns the rest of us who are not in those roles.

On college campuses in North America, we are more divided than any time that I can remember. Perhaps not on exactly these issues at the moment, but on other issues, we could do something that would involve listening to each other, trying to ask and to hear: what does this mean for you? We could be curious, locating the judgment parts of the conversation not at the beginning – at least, not leading with that.

I think this is true for people who live in Israel and live in Gaza, many of whom have long known each other as neighbors. And yet they haven't found a way to actually interact. This is true in Europe, too. There are people I know in France who are having exactly this problem with neighbors. They can't even talk to each other. So, I return to my question from before: who is the "we" in these questions? Once we locate, we identify, that the "we" includes some people who are neighbors and have had things in common in the past, I think that these steps are very, very relevant.

I've had fascinating opportunities to watch up close as people emerging from terrible conflicts take those small steps, whether it's through a formal process like a Truth and Reconciliation Commission or it's by cooperating around some shared goal, like building a community center. And those are steps that people can take and actually do take if they see a common ground, if they see some reason to have common ground.

One of the terrible features of the tragic Israel-Gaza story is that we have a not just recent but longstanding history of leaders who don't want a solution, leaders for whom the investment in the conflict is part of their own personal power. As long as that's the case, we can't have these steps, and it will take other people who say "no more!" and change who the leaders are.

Irene

That's a very sobering thought because as Katja Donovan mentioned at the beginning of this conversation [February 2024], several major parts of the world are facing elections soon, and the choices seem to be between candidates, as you put it just now, Martha, who don't seem to want resolution and those who maybe do want resolution and do want to work together.

Liz, you travel and work with so many different types of people. How do you see this "scaling up" happening? Is there something that the little folk – which is definitely what I'm feeling like right now: very little! – is there something that I need to be doing to create the path towards the scaling up of these wonderful practices that you've shared with us?

Liz

I share with Martha the sense that it's just so big! What I might propose is small. Martha has guided me in the past at difficult moments, and your book, Martha, *Between Vengeance and Forgiveness* (1999) to me is one of the most powerful books I have ever read. You specifically helped me through a couple of projects by showing me some ways – I don't want to just say of hope, it's more of practice. It's a way to practice the thing, including what you did during our project, *Small Dances about Big Ideas*, in relationship to the Truth and Reconciliation Commission.

Arizona State University, where I've been teaching, is an amazing place, but it scales up constantly the whole idea: scale up, scale up, scale up, scale up, scale big, scale big! There are fruits from that in terms of access. We have so many more people at my university who wouldn't be there or at other schools either. Inclusion is key to our school. And these people are doing amazing things. There are so many students from around the world and you can see through them ways of opening it up. But there is also the other scale, that is, the microscopic, and that also is really important to figure out.

Martha, you've talked about a couple who is distraught [in an opening example]. That could seem microscopic and yet it, too, is important. This situation in Gaza right now is so horrible for somebody like myself, an American Jew, and for you, Martha, an American Jew. I think this is in part why my new project, *My Body is a Library*, feels so true to me. When the patriarch Abraham died, his two sons are in that cave with him, and the questions I keep asking are: Were they already on distinct paths? Were they already separating their burial practices from each other? How early did this separation start? I feel like I'm living with that question in my body. Not at the political level, but in a visceral way. I believe that the body, the way we feel and express, if we give it an opportunity, along with our imaginations, it can help us hold ambiguity in a way that words often cannot. I know that those hearing or reading me might think they don't understand this, but actually we do it all the time: we allow ourselves to feel joy, grief, confusion, anger, and to consider how we might live with these emotions while having ideas at the same time. So often, we have to separate them, but in truth, if we let our bodies, minds, and dare I say, souls, speak to us, we can have a sensibility about something without always starting or ending with words. I call this "dwelling on something," and it is both a verb and a noun and also a place. On another level, I think that we can be making connections, working through things.

I agree with you, Martha, that strategy with our students is helping them de-escalate the controversy at this moment. I am concerned by the speed with which we are talking to each other about our differences and our opinions. And I am concerned with the positions that we assume and hold. I might think of this as we allow the anger and the opinion to form a shape, and then we are stuck in it. My suggestion is to allow some space for moving into other shapes. It's scary because while we are in momentum of change, we might not be so sure of everything. That is partly its beauty. But you can always assume your old shape (of an idea or a position), or perhaps find a nuance that changes it a lot or a little.

Critical Response Process can help with this through its practice of turning discomfort to inquiry as we discussed and trying to get to a neutral question. Both of these things help de-escalate the situation. Another concerns the speed with which the anger comes up. That's another thing Critical Response Process can help with, a de-escalation.

What a horrible place for us to be in, as Martha has just described, with our leadership. Personally, speaking out every day, I don't see how killing innocent people gets us anywhere. I just don't. It is terrible to see the state of Israel, born as it was, coming out of what it did, and it not being able to treat others differently. I know I'm not living there, and I didn't lose my family on October 7. But I am willing to work on it here.

Martha

I'm thinking right now about the words that make up the name of this conversation series: "Humanities for Humans." They make me reflect that I am drawn constantly to that basic question. If we're dealing with humans, isn't that something that we have in common, that we are human? Can't being human be a starting point for connection? I'd like to add one thing about that extraordinary group "Doctors Without Borders" that was in Rwanda on the ground as the genocide was unfurling. The local head, Dr. James Orbinski, anticipated that all of the children who were being housed in a hospital were at risk of violence. So, he went to the head of the hospital, and he said to him, "you know, I fear that the machetes are coming. It's terrible! We have to get these children to safety." And the doctor said to Orbinski, "No, we can't do that." So, Orbinski said to the doctor, "Are you a parent?" And immediately, the man opened up his wallet where he had pictures of his children. He was obviously very proud of them. And then Dr. Orbinski said, "Well, these are children, too! They're somebody's child." The head of the hospital responded to that, "No, they're cockroaches." It was in fact that word and similar words in Rwanda, similar words during the Holocaust, similar words in Vietnam, similar words in Gaza. It's this demeaning subordination of human beings to being not human that allows people to do horrific things. So, yes! I do think it's absolutely critical to resist that, to insist on recognizing people as humans. Talking about scale, at least I can start with my own communications, with how I talk.

Liz

I would like to thank you for that, too, Martha. If people see the film "Origin" about Isabel Wilkerson or read her book *Caste* (2020), they will see and feel even more of what you were just speaking about. In this context, I want to mention my own inability to celebrate Hanukkah this past year [2023]. I couldn't even light the candles. I just couldn't do it. But I did write eight "Miracles." And I'd like to mention them here. I have been told that they feel like Afro-Futurism. Maybe. I was aided in writing by Martha and by my daughter Anna and her husband Peter, who is German. They live in Turkey, and he works for UNESCO in Afghanistan, so they also see things from differing world situations. Some of what is written there has been on my mind for a very long time. Some of it arose after October 7. Hanukkah's arrival, with its ritual candle lighting, gift giving, and storytelling of resistance, became the torment and the structure for me to imagine these hopes. And yes, even miracles.

Here it is:
This year, instead of candles, I am observing a miracle a day.

Day One: The people awaken to a world without soldiers in their midst. They look for fuel as they rebuild their homes, their hospitals, their streets. And behold! Although there is only enough fuel for one day, what they have lasts 8 days, long enough to get what they need from the rest of the world.

Day Two: The families awake and find all prisoners and all hostages are walking towards home. Everyone has been fed and is safe.

Day Three: The miraculous return of those raped to death, their pelvises now intact, their heads are back on their bodies, which bear no bruises from having been dragged through the streets. The bodies torn apart by bomb after bomb are back in place, where they were put by God, Allah, Buddha, the Divine Sacred.

Day Four: Leaders of States and Governments realize they can't fight a proxy war with their enemy by killing thousands of innocents. They agree to meet with all sides.

Day Five: The people realize they have been misled by their government, a government led by a man who must prosecute this war or lose his power and possibly be imprisoned; a government that ignored the warnings because the military was too arrogant to believe resistance could be organized and too macho to listen to a woman who forecast these devastating events. And, so, the people elect a government devoted to a two-state solution and living side by side.

Day Six: In the United States, the American people decide to de-escalate their opinions and try listening. In Congress, in academia, in families, in religious institutions, and within ourselves. Each one of us realizing that we are in relation and in community.

Day Seven: We understand that we have to share the land, nurture its beauty, and find a way to identify our heritage, our cultures, and our beings beyond what we own.

Day Eight: All the candles are lit. A song of permanent cease fire is heard everywhere; there is prayer, dancing, gatherings, of political or religious nature. And all the children feel safe for the first time in years. The children can sleep now. They can rest in the arms of their mothers and fathers. The children can go to school and to the movies without fear, holding the hands of their siblings or their friends. The war machines that pretended to be in their interests have been halted. A new psalm is written in which the music itself, and the way it beats in our hearts and our muscles, tells us that we can live with our differences.

The thing about the "Miracles" in the way I intended them involves not denying the horror of the present, but also posing what it could be. I suppose there's a bit of naivete there, though it isn't like I say, "Here is how you do it." It did help that I could at least imagine it.

Martha

Imagination is so important. It's absolutely critical to think that it's possible, that it could be otherwise. I always communicate to my law students how critical it is to study history, to study comparatively what other countries do and have done. Science fiction is important for the same reason. To imagine other worlds is the strength of human beings. That's what we can do even in the darkest times!

Irene

To repeat some of your important thoughts, Liz and Martha: one thing we can do is treat those around us as human beings. That seems truly fundamental. Another is to imagine. Perhaps I can share that we focused on the importance of the imagination in an earlier conversation of "Humanities for Humans." The general topic was climate change. But in talking together before the public conversation where we had to narrow it down, the experts shared how central to them the idea of imagining a new future for the earth is, a future that could be liveable for humans and animals and plants. So that's exactly what we called it: "Imagining Anew the Future of the Earth." Rebecca Tsosie, a philosopher and legal scholar from Arizona, who also does Native American studies, and Harriet Hawkins, a British cultural geographer who often works with artists, insisted, each from their own experience and disciplines, on how critical it is to imagine that things could be different. Because if you can't imagine that it could be different, then we don't really have a chance of getting there. I think that's what both of you are saying about controversy, disagreement, outright aggression. To add one more thought, there was a very controversial piece in *The New Yorker* a few years back by the author Jonathan Safran Foer, who was arguing that it's definitely too late to save the planet, but that doesn't mean we should give up and not do anything. He urged individuals to find a project that means something to you, a project that you can do something about. So, if there's a park you love and they're threatening to turn it into a parking lot, then you can fight for that spot of green in your neighborhood. To connect this with what we've been talking about here today, I wonder if that's also a hope that we can offer listeners. Can you practice these steps? Can you practice non-judgment? Can you practice respect? Can you speak from experience rather than from authority? Can we be practicing all of that in situations over which we might have a modicum of control? That might just be a good idea no matter what, but perhaps I also want to have the hope that if a lot of us try to follow the steps we've been talking about, our efforts will add up to some different, some more peaceful spirit in the world. Am I being an unrealistic optimist at this point?

Martha

I totally agree that hope is critical. Taking steps, action often seems more feasible, more imaginable, more doable when it's local, when it's small. Your comments make me recall that when Al Gore created the film about why environmental challenges overwhelm people[2], he noticed that – and he is so powerful on this point – people move very quickly either to denial or to feeling overwhelmed. It's too big and therefore there's nothing I can do, and pessimism takes over. It seems to me that the challenge is to manage our feelings so that we *can* imagine, so that we *can* act. I want to return to your comments about fear, Liz. We can turn it into a resource as opposed to shutting down.

Liz

I want us not to skip over something: I think we even have to *practice* imagination. The topics and steps we've been discussing are so powerful, so effective, and yet, it's fascinating to me how little we train in them. I have a short essay proposing that Einstein was a choreographer because he was so good at thought experiments. Through his thought experiments, he was living in his imagination. When I studied that a bit, it felt similar to the way I live in my imagination when I'm in the midst of making something. I can sit there and spend enormous amounts

---

2 Editor's note: *An Inconvenient Truth* (2006).

of time in my imagination. It's like a giant computer because I can delete, add, subtract.

Let me try restating that: imagination is a practice. And like any other type of practice, there are warm-ups. There are things you know. You keep at it so that in times of need, you don't have to wait for it to come unbidden. You actually have it. Here we go once more. Let me try this formulation: it is a tool; it is part of who you are. With regard to not having the garden be turned into a parking lot, there are many things you need to have practiced. I have to get out of bed and actually do something. I can't let myself be a pessimist today. I've got to talk to my neighbor. I've got to pick up the person who doesn't have a car. Or maybe you're riding a bike instead of being in a car. To my sense of it, just saying all of those things counts towards building the kind of world that we want to be in. And yet so often we dismiss them as too insignificant, or we just completely overlook them.

There's one other point floating out there about judgment. It's not so much about being non-judgmental. Rather, I'm interested in how we turn judgment into inquiry. When do we engage with our judgment because our judgment is telling us something is wrong? We could think of it and emotion like a signal: I'm sad. I'm happy. I'm this. I'm that. That's a signal where the next step can be to quickly move to inquiry – something you can practice! You can use those questions to get us somewhere. After teaching critical response all these years, I count judgments like neutrinos. They're coming at us every second, and we're having them every second. So, the issue really is how we manage them. Manage is a good term you use, Martha. It's such a good point related to practice.

Martha

Elaine Scarry is a professor of English at Harvard who wrote a book called *Thinking in an Emergency* (2011). It could have been a short book with two words: you can't. But instead, it's a beautiful book that talks about the fact that since you can't think in an emergency, you have to practice ahead of time – which is exactly right. And then you have it available.

It is striking to me that young people today actually need more practice in having conversations, more practice in knowing how to separate out the question from the statement, and in how to read the emotions of the other person. To put it yet another way: how to be in the presence of another person who has emotions. I don't know whether that was always true for the young, but it seems to me like there's more need for actual practice of those kinds of activities. A study coming out of MIT indicated that undergraduates would prefer on the whole to have asynchronous communications, because then they don't have to manage the feelings that somebody else has.

Irene

I can certainly say as a teacher myself for many decades that things have changed in terms of students' ability to talk to adults. The pandemic didn't help any, because students were able to – often told to do many things asynchronously, and in general, face to face conversations have become more and more rare for the younger generation. They'd much rather text about arranging even what they're going to do that evening with their friends, for instance. This is not a criticism of the younger generation. Martha already brought it up. It's the very structure of digital communications.

Communication itself has changed so much and instead of just bemoaning that, we could use it as a call to all of us who are in teaching positions about how important it is to help our students learn those skills you've both talked about. To make them aware of and help them acquire the tools they'll need in life and to urge them to practice using those tools.

Liz

I'm working on something right now called, "The Atlas of Creative Tools." It's not public yet, but I'm hoping to make it a place where people can access all kinds of things. What I really want to say is that people already have their own tools, but they just don't realize that. Sometimes they'll call it intuition. I think your intuition is your knowledge arriving super-fast. If you do a kind of deep reflection when you're inspired, you can go one more step and ask what it was that inspired you about this thing or situation, and then you'll hear yourself say the thing that you want to practice. In any case, I do believe that most people have a lot of tools. So, I'd like to urge people: Go back over a situation when you were saving yourself, a moment that happened and then you got out of it. You saved yourself! Fabulous! Well, what did you do exactly? Those are the tools that will be of use. It's a mentality around that that I call a toolbox mentality, or maybe better would be an Atlas mentality.

Irene

This is intriguing. Could you continue explaining what you mean?

Liz

It goes like this: Each person can develop what I might call a toolbox mentality, and by that, I mean that whether you're working intuitively, or with recipes, or with processes that someone has taught you, you can be paying attention to the things that work, to the way you interchange them, and you will come to find that it's actually interesting to make your own toolbox, your own set of ways of working. Sometimes I think of it like this: I can teach you how to swim. We can walk slowly into the pool, and we can start practicing our breathing, and then we can practice our movements and our kicking. We do all the things to become good swimmers, working from the shallow end to a point where suddenly you're in the deep end and you're swimming. That's one way to think about a toolbox.

But what I'm calling a toolbox mentality would be something like this: I'd throw you in the deep end and let's pretend that you don't know how to swim. You would start thrashing around and you might notice that if you cup your hands, you can keep your head up longer. You might notice the speed of how much you're working your arms. You might notice that if you add your legs, you can keep your head above water. You might even notice that keeping your head above water is a good idea. This is really how the toolbox mentality works. It's you noticing that you're in the deep end. Things are happening. You're surviving.

Irene

Maybe this is my idealism again, but is there anything we need to say before we close about love?

Martha

I suppose that's a part of recognizing other humans' rights. But love is a tall order. I don't think it could be commanded. Maybe this is the context to reflect on the experience I had after having a child and suddenly realizing that for everybody alive who is a human being, some mother went through this process of pregnancy and birth for them. That certainly is something I hold on to, even when I'm having a difficult conversation with someone. Somebody went through a lot for you to be around!

I relate this to the idea of a mediator, the conviction that sometimes you can't do it alone. Sometimes you need somebody else to help orchestrate the conversation, to set the ground rules, to make sure that everyone is treated fairly and has an equal opportunity, and sometimes even an adjudicator, someone who will resolve a conflict.

I do think that there are practices that everyone can engage in related to playing those kinds of roles in their own lives and being willing to have in essence a social contract that says: we have a conflict and we're going to have to solve it, and we're going to agree to solve it this way.

Liz

That's a helpful train of thought, Martha. I used to think that everybody understood that you see this over here and apply it over there. Over time, I've come to realize that's not the case. Rather, again, it's a matter of practice: How do I make this make sense to me over here? Make sense of another context? For another purpose?

Trying to put our conversation together with love makes me think of the work we did with veterans over a number of months during the 150th anniversary of the American Civil War. We built a piece around what was happening in Iran and Iraq, that is, with veterans returning from that war. One of the things I learned by talking to so many of them, and by being in circles with them, is that there seemed to be three things that had happened to them. Why they would sign up to serve again was not because of our political policies. They reenlisted because there's a certain amount of risk, and risk is a wonderful thing. What I mean is that risk can keep you on the edge. I happen to love risk, too. But they also had purpose. The third thing was love. They didn't always use the word love, but it was so clear that they loved their comrades, as did my father. The only time he would talk about World War II was in relationship to this kind of love of comrades. I don't think we do such a good job of expanding the notion of what we mean by love to encompass the kind of love these veterans felt.

Even in my classrooms, I want my students to sit there and love each other in a manner in which they can support each other's ups and downs, growth experiences, changes, and all that. You can create that kind of world; truly you can. It's helped by watching them. They have taught me so much when I listen to or witness the ways in which supporting each other played out for them. Critical Response helps in giving folks the skills for this. But, also, I have noticed how important it is for me to help them understand competition and inspiration. If you insist on living in a vertical world, where you are constantly climbing upwards, then, when someone else shows something that you admire, your only choice is to feel bad because yours is worse, or you push harder to out-compete them. If you live in the horizontal, you have another set of choices. Instead of saying, "Wow, I could never do that," you ask yourself, "Wow, what was it about that which inspired me?" And here is where a toolbox mentality can help, because you can discern the process, the tool, or a way of thinking and borrow that. It's a way of turning inspiration into a workroom, a rehearsal, or something to try out. It's very exciting.

Irene

We have a question from the audience, from someone who's listening to us from Tel Aviv. They write: "I thought it" – I assume they mean this conversation – "would be neutral, but the only condemnation was uttered about Israel. Why doesn't anyone condemn the atrocities of Hamas?" This person continues on about academia and that they've been reading about Jewish students, even those who are not espousing Zionism, being attacked by anti-Israel mobs and asks: "can't you influence the authorities to prevent demonstrations and sponsor only discussions at which academics of various persuasions will encourage information?"

I don't know which universities this listener is referring to, but at Dartmouth College where I teach, I am very fortunate to have colleagues who immediately – literally on October 7 – got in touch with each other, professors of Middle Eastern and Arabic studies and Jewish studies. They realized right away how important it would be to have discussions with students, to "encourage and give information" in the context of our community as a university, a place where we are located to learn. They also understood emotions would be running very high. So, two big public forums occurred at Dartmouth within days of the Hamas attacks. I was so impressed not only with the amount of information, of teaching my colleagues did during these forums, but also with their own modeling of calm discussion, and their own reflexes to de-escalate whenever a student got up and starting yelling. I am confused about our listener's perception that only the atrocities of Israel are talked about here and also the perception that only Jewish students are having problems feeling safe right now. That's not what I'm reading and hearing.

Martha

I should have been more explicit when I said recognizing the humanity of others. I certainly mean the hostages, too. And I certainly mean the Israelis who were killed, whether they were at a concert or they were at home in a kibbutz. I am appalled when I look at groups that claim to be feminists who deny that rapes happened. So, when I say it's important to recognize the humanity of others, I mean that too. I am absolutely outraged that there are people on my campus tearing down posters with photos of the hostages. That's a perfect example of what I was trying to describe about not recognizing the humanity of other human beings, of treating them as cockroaches. The fact of someone taking down the poster is an acknowledgement that "oh my goodness, someone might actually recognize that these hostages are human beings, and I don't want that." I am sympathetic to the listener's question about why we can't have discussions about the issues rather than protests.

To be sure, we have a very strong commitment to free speech in this country, and that includes on college campuses. I myself have been a big advocate of what we call "time, place, and manner" restrictions. I do not believe that there should be protests where people are eating or sleeping or studying. That's consistent in my view with the rules that apply to public spaces. I believe they should apply to even private campuses. It is tough; it is tough. There are so many strong, strong feelings right now. Some people just don't seem to be ready to have conversations. I would also comment that whatever is being said and done seems to be going in all directions, not just one. There's been a lot of anti-Islamism as well as antisemitism.

Liz

I feel for the person who wrote in that question. I don't know that this is adequate, but I mentioned earlier, the eight days of Miracles that I wrote during Hanukkah. It may not meet the desires of the listener, but on day three, I wrote of the miraculous return of those raped to death. In my miracle, their pelvises are now intact; their heads are back on their bodies, which bear no bruises from having been dragged through the streets; the bodies torn apart by bomb after bomb are back in place where they were put by God, by Allah, by Buddha or by the Divine Sacred.

In this example, you see me again framing bigger and yet still trying to include the specifics and the horrors of what happened.

Irene

This is obviously a very sober place to be winding down this conversation, but I think in coming together today, we all were aware that this is a very difficult time we're living through – on campuses, but of course all over the world (and we haven't mentioned most of the armed conflicts that are currently occurring). It's a main reason I wanted to have you in conversation with the public. We're in a very, very sobering moment in human history, it seems to me, where people are grasping at violence rather than seeing someone else's humanity. Many countries, unfortunately, have leaders who do not want resolutions, as you pointed out earlier, Martha. That is something perhaps each of us in societies like ours that still make claims for marginal freedom of speech and elections should think about. What does it mean to be supporting leaders who don't want resolution? And what are the different kinds of resolutions that are available to us that no one is talking about? We have to work in whatever ways possible for conversations that might lead to resolutions being put in place.

Martha

I was very helped by Liz's suggestion, both in talking about critical response steps, but also steps in general for helping each of us to separate out things that we just immediately combine. As an example, I've worked on and written quite a lot about the issue of forgiveness. I think that it's absolutely critical to separate out the acts of forgiveness from honoring and recognizing people's justified sense of outrage and resentment being violated.

Forgiveness, whatever it is, is an aspiration that's embraced by every religion, by every philosophic tradition. It means letting go of a justified resentment. But, first, let's recognize the justified resentment.

Liz

I love that, Martha. You've shared that with me before, and I'm really glad for you to raise that again. It's really, really good, as are the four definitions of truth that you brought to my attention that the Truth and Reconciliation Commission used in order to do that excruciatingly difficult work in South Africa.

Martha

I can mention them here. The South African Truth and Reconciliation Commission very powerfully articulated that there are different kinds of truth. It's not relativism to acknowledge that there are forensic truths, the truths of personal narrative, social truth that emerges from dialogue, and there's truth that is constructed in healing processes. They are not the same, and they are all important.

Irene

That is an inspiring place to suspend this conversation.

Marianne Hirsch
Reparative Memory in Practice

Marianne Hirsch and I have collaborated in so many ways that it would take pages for me to list them all here. We were institutional colleagues from my arrival at Dartmouth in 1994 until her departure for Columbia in 2004; we have collaborated and continued our friendship up to the present. Marianne included me in many things she was doing when I was a newly arrived assistant professor, to mention just two: inviting me to participate in a marvelously generative seminar on "memory and gender," and to co-edit a volume on "Teaching the Representation of the Holocaust" for the widely circulated "Options for Teaching" series of the Modern Language Association. The faith she and other members of the Dartmouth Comparative Literature program had to assign me the linchpin class on literary and critical theory was a big boost in my coming to believe that maybe I had something intellectual to offer the community and the profession. When I was struggling to complete my first book, Marianne told me: it just gets easier. It was hard to believe her at the time, but she was right. I mentioned earlier in this volume (in my own biographical sketch) that Marianne's concept of postmemory was enormously helpful to me in understanding some of my own childhood experiences as well as challenges related to my work with stories of my father's war experiences. I have admired so many things about Marianne and how she has conducted her career; I'll cite here her monumentally generative contribution to the field of memory studies through her term "postmemory"; her mentoring, especially of younger colleagues; her frequent and enormously productive collaborations with her life partner, Leo Spitzer; and her seemingly boundless energy, honesty, and courage that have allowed her to query her own concepts and those of others. I will close myself down now by saying: it's hard to imagine how the field of memory studies would have developed and would be still developing without her contributions. Similarly, it is hard to imagine what career I would have had without inspiration and support from Marianne.

Here is what Marianne Hirsch would like to share about her path.

I feel fortunate to have done my Ph.D. studies in Comparative Literature in the early 1970s, during the rise of second wave feminism. When I began teaching at Dartmouth College, I helped found the first Women's Studies Program in the Ivy League, and I started writing about women writers and, specifically, about mother-daughter relationships in literature by women – what Adrienne Rich called "the great unwritten story." This interest in family narratives led me to the subject of family memory and how it is passed down across generations. Drawing on my own family experience of surviving the Holocaust, I came to the emerging field of "Memory Studies" and the process of transgenerational memory of traumatic histories that I have termed "postmemory." My work on memory has been dedicated to creating a space for small stories that might otherwise remain absent from the historical record.

My books include *The Mother-Daughter Plot: Narrative, Psychoanalysis, Feminism* (1989), *Family Frames: Photography, Narrative and Postmemory* (1997), *The Generation of Postmemory: Writing and Visual Culture After the Holocaust* (2012). I co-authored *Ghosts of Home: The Afterlife of Czernowitz in Jewish Memory* (2010) and *School Photos in Liquid Time: Reframing Difference* (2020) with Leo Spitzer. My edited and co-edited volumes include *Teaching the Representation of the Holocaust*, co-edited with Irene Kacandes (2004), *The Familial Gaze* (1998), *Women Mobilizing Memory* (2019), and *Imagining Everyday Life* (2021). I am professor emerita in Comparative Literature and Gender Studies at Columbia University in New York, a former President of the Modern Language Association of America and a member of the American Academy of Arts and Sciences. I have always loved to collaborate and co-create spaces where scholars, artists and activists can work together on projects of common

Figure 1: "Imagine Repair," Projection by the Illuminator, April 23, 2022, Cathedral of St. John the Divine, New York City, photo by Desirée Rios.

interest. In that spirit, I co-founded Columbia University's Center for the Study of Social Difference, where with a group of colleagues, I initiated the Zip Code Memory Project: Practices of Justice and Repair, dedicated to finding community-based ways to memorialize the devastating losses resulting from the Coronavirus pandemic while also acknowledging its radically differential effects on Upper New York City neighborhoods. I am currently working on a book about reparative memory.

And here is the contribution she makes to our volume.

Trauma and repair

How can individuals and communities repair long-standing legacies of structural inequality and violence and their traumatic after-effects? This question became urgent for me as I lived through the Covid-19 pandemic in New York City. For the last three decades, I have worked on the memory of the Holocaust and other catastrophic histories, yet the reparative potentials of memory – the possibility of healing and repair – were not my primary concerns. My goal was to trace and to understand the workings of trauma and its transmission across generations.

It's not surprising that in listening to survivors of the Holocaust and other catastrophic histories, we would come to understand the long arc of trauma and its perpetuating repetition and reactivation. I found that although trauma, literally, is a wound to the flesh and, metaphorically, to the psyche that resides in the individual body, it can be, and is, transmitted to others, even others who were not there to experience the events that occasioned it. This is what I have discussed as "postmemory" – the legacy of traumatic histories that reach across geographies and generations. The testimonies that survivors transmit, whether in the form of stories, literature, art, or simply behaviors, require attentive listening and modes of retelling that are ethical and non-appropriative. When memory scholars and practitioners bring such neglected and forgotten stories into public memory, we aim to reshape the ways in which history is written. But in view of continuing racism, antisemitism, political neglect, and injustice, trauma and memory studies also aim to do more: they can become platforms for demands for historical accountability, justice, and reparation. If trauma reaches across generations, affecting not only survivors but also descendants and their descendants, the claim for reparation and justice becomes even more urgent.

And yet, in recent years, for me and many of my colleagues, doing work on memory within the unforgiving frame and teleology of trauma – the powerful idea that it will repeat, and can never truly be healed – has come to feel constraining. I've had the occasion to study the workings of social and cultural memory in the context of several transnational interdisciplinary working groups and to participate in memory networks and conferences in numerous locations across the globe. Inspired by feminist, queer, de-colonial, and Indigenous ideas about time and memory and by commitments to social justice, some of these groups have displaced the focus on trauma and its inexorable after-effects. I have joined them in examining alternative, multiple, non-linear ideas about time and memory that help to reveal aspects of the past and its continuing presence that resist the inevitability of trauma and its unforgiving return. Without denying the magnitude of traumatic loss, the focus on vulnerability, care, mutual aid, and repair can help us reveal instances of resistance and refusal in the past, and also of hope and belief in a future.

The zip code memory project

This impulse to think seriously about what might make healing and some forms of repair and justice possible in the wake of traumatic histories was sharpened for me during the Covid-19 pandemic – especially in the part of New York City where I live and work and where the losses caused by the pandemic are so unevenly and unjustly distributed. In the Spring of 2021, I was part of a small group of academics, artists and activists who sought reparative ways to acknowledge these devastating losses and to memorialize the people, institutions, moments, and places that our communities lost. How, we wondered, can we account for and how can we bridge the gap between the depth of personal and familial loss and the magnitude of collective, communal, national and global loss, all unequally experienced? It is thus that we conceived the Zip Code Memory Project.[1]

Performance Studies scholar Diana Taylor, photographers and artists Susan Meiselas and Lorie Novak, American and Gender Studies scholar Laura Wexler and I had devoted much of our careers to working with trauma and painful pasts in different parts of the world, most recently in a transnational feminist working group and book project *Women Mobilizing Memory*.[2] But, now, with Covid raging,

---

[1] The Zip Code Memory Project was collaboratively conceived and realized which poses challenges to writing about it. My descriptions and reflections owe a great deal to multiple conversations and draw, in some parts, on the prose of grant applications and the zcmp.org website that were co-written, in particular, with project co-director Diana Taylor.

[2] Ayşe Gül Altınay, María José Contreras, Marianne Hirsch, Jean Howard, Banu Karaca, Alisa Solomon, eds., *Women Mobilizing Memory*, Columbia University Press, 2019.

with Black Lives Matter gaining energy, what about our own city? Could local networks of care and mutual aid that were sustaining our neighbors be extended to create a larger communal space to commemorate and mourn the losses, devise practices of repair, and articulate demands for justice? What, in these circumstances, could *we* do, as academics and artists with some access to funding by universities and foundations?

Individually and together, the five of us organizers had contributed to what we conceived as practice-based feminist memory work. Could what we learned in our feminist transnational projects be brought to bear on this moment, in this local context? An attentiveness to difference, the work of active listening, building solidarity, and embracing unknowing, a vigilance about our own complicity and implication in social structures of inequality – all these were sure to be useful here. So would our feminist commitments to bring small individual and communal stories of dailiness to light, in the belief that when memory activates the past in a communal setting, it can also reframe it and help us imagine a different potential ending – one that can serve as a provocation for collective political engagement. Thus, perhaps, memory could be reparative and oriented toward the future.

Acknowledgment and commemoration, we believe, are necessary steps in collective action and repair. For over two years, New York individuals and families had been engaged in mourning their losses, but the work of communal, national, and global remembrance was just beginning, and threatened to be stalled by pandemic fatigue. Communities were living with the losses they had suffered, even as all of us were still urged to keep a safe distance from each other and were unable to gather, mourn, process, and organize together. What, we in our group asked ourselves, does togetherness mean, what does community mean, when the virus revealed radical economic and thus also health-related inequalities in our social landscapes? How, in these circumstances, can we rebuild, or, rather, build sustainable communities that can work toward – and demand – justice and repair? Clearly, this global moment of momentous injury and failure, and of shared vulnerability, would require its very own commemorative paradigms: it did not seem as though the past could usefully guide us, except perhaps through the specter of rapid forgetting as exemplified by the 1918 flu epidemic. As we began to build our project, we saw that we would have to unlearn as much as learn.

The area we focused on (Upper Manhattan, Harlem, Washington Heights, and the South Bronx) comprised lands belonging to the Indigenous Lenape people. It attests to a history of repeated dispossession and inequality as well as resistance and renewal. We thought of using Zip Codes as the clearest markers of the uneven distribution of prosperity, precarity, and hope in these neighborhoods. Zip Codes that house larger Black, Latinx, and undocumented populations have suffered far greater losses of subsistence, health, education, and life and have seen the greatest infection and mortality rates. Crowded apartments and the inability to work from home compounded these effects. Women, especially, were called on to offer disproportionate amounts of care during this moment, losing jobs and livelihood, and the disabled lost essential support. In Judith Butler's terms, these neighborhoods are marked by the deep social divide between lives that are "grievable" and lives that are not. The vast legacies of systemic inequality and neglect that the pandemic revealed so starkly across the Zip Codes in which we live and work demanded accountability and transformation. Those of us organizing this project believed that economic recovery after the pandemic would fall short without the communal work of taking stock, of mourning, acknowledgment, and memory that are necessary parts of personal and social recovery. But, at the same time, we believed that memory work also needs to be accompanied by a continued struggle for social and economic justice.

When we applied for funding to the Henry Luce Foundation and to Columbia University, we suggested that this project might be able to offer a space in which the work of repair could be envisioned. We knew that the need was immediate, and we feared that, if we waited, the impulse to move on and forget would obviate this opportunity for recognition and working through. The vast legacies of systemic failure, inequality, and neglect that the pandemic revealed so starkly demanded accountability and transformation. But it became clear that, once over, the pandemic might be quickly forgotten as communities would be urged to go back to "normal," even as "normal" had come to seem unacceptable. How to make space for memory work, for an acknowledgment of traumatic loss that would nevertheless interrupt the arc of its repetition?

Animated by our trust in the transformative power of art and community, we envisioned that combining writing, art, and theater practices with broad-based theoretical understandings of trauma, grief, and body memory, might help our communities re-imagine Zip Codes not as zones of separation, but as interrelated spaces for connectivity and mutual care. The effects of lockdown and isolation, we realized, would need the healing power of physical proximity –connection, community, and touch. We hoped that sharing memories through creative activities could forge meaningful paths of connection through the sustaining potential of togetherness. We searched for new ways to be together and to build a process of accompaniment – of seeing, listening, acknowledging and, where possible, addressing past wrongs and alleviating present pain in creative, even joyful ways.

As organizers, we began by building a team of talented and dedicated multilingual workshop leaders, curators, filmmakers, and Public Humanities graduate student fellows from several area universities who would help us conceive the project. Together, we spent the summer of 2021 meeting repeatedly with commu-

Reparative Memory in Practice —— 147

Figure 2: Rehearsals for Change Workshop with George Emilio Sanchez, Fall 2021, New York City. Photo by Desirée Rios.

nity and arts organizations, churches, and public educational institutions to learn how they had weathered the pandemic and to engage them as partners.[3] With their help, we invited a group of community members to join several months of art-based workshops and public events devoted to co-creating community, trust, and hope. The project was designed to be small – a pilot of sorts, replicable in other places, but not in itself expansive. Between 40 and 50 participants joined our team of over 20, and, while some dropped out after a few sessions, others came into the project later and stayed on. Participants ranged in age from 18 to 80; they were students, teachers, nurses, social workers, artists, curators, community leaders, and activists; they represented the full diversity of these neighborhoods in terms of race, gender, national origin, and ethnicity. Many were recent immigrants. Some were retired and living alone, others busy parents and professionals. A smaller core group of enthusiastic participants was instrumental in building the project and its activities.

Over the course of nine months, from fall 2021 to spring 2022, we all came together in a series of programs that addressed the losses of the pandemic and aimed

---

[3] https://zcmp.org/partners/.

to imagine paths of hope. From the first meetings on, this diverse group of strangers joined to create a space where we could come together, even as new variants and renewed lockdowns repeatedly made it challenging to gather in person.

The Zip Code Memory Project had several concurrent dimensions as well as a temporal arc. A series of small-group art-based workshops over the fall of 2021 culminated in a large community-wide "Gathering for Covid" at the Cathedral of St. John the Divine, with a candle-light vigil, public testimonials, and a performance by the Sing Harlem Choir.[4] These first months, we thought, would be devoted to allowing ourselves to feel what we had experienced and what we had lost, that is, to remembering, mourning, and healing. And we hoped that in the second part of the project, additional small writing and art workshops, as well as an exhibition[5] and a series of presentations and performances[6] would engage both our participants and a large public to work toward demanding justice as well as imagining repair.

To imagine what kinds of commemorative practices and structures might be best suited to this particular historical catastrophe, we also invited known memorial artists whose work with communities in different parts of the world had inspired us to participate in two virtual roundtables on "Reparative Memory." Additional virtual roundtables on "Why Zip Codes?" and "Chronic Life: Can We Go the Distance With the Virus?" brought demographers, geographers, public health and medical humanities experts into the conversation.[7] Additionally, with our twelve Public Humanities fellows, we formed a reading and discussion group about the work we were doing on the ground. It is here that the most trenchant questioning and critiques of the project emerged: questions about our presence, as mostly white academics, in these diverse communities; about our bringing workshops to them rather than doing the slow work of allowing activities to evolve more organically from within; about our privilege and ways to acknowledge it, and more.

Practicing repair

As the project and these discussions progressed, a few key concepts emerged and evolved. Let me say a few words, specifically, about *repair* and the ways in which it has helped us organize the project. In its most common usage, *reparation* is a

---

4 https://zcmp.org/gatherings/.
5 https://zcmp.org/exhibition/.
6 https://zcmp.org/imagine-repair-april-may-2022/.
7 https://zcmp.org/roundtables/.

political and legal concept – a public acknowledgment of injury by a state or state-connected institution, and a compensatory settlement that often, but not always, involves a financial compensation. The accent here is on injury and on acknowledgment: reparation and repair entail a recognition that something is broken, that someone has been wronged.

Reparation is also an operative concept in psychoanalysis, particularly in object relations theory inspired by Melanie Klein's revisions of Freud and her pioneering practical and theoretical work in infant and child psychology.[8] Klein's thinking is important, I believe, because she traces the ambivalences in early infant object relations between mother and child, the impulses to repair the relationships of care that, as infants, we imagine we have ourselves destroyed through our contradictory feelings. Klein enables us to see our own implication in loss and death and to recognize that the work of mourning is, in itself, a process of reparation. Her focus on mother-infant relationships reveals the profound entanglement we have and continue to have with one another as humans. This entanglement becomes all the more palpable in our era of global contagion where individual, communal, and national boundaries are ever more permeable; where even our breath and touch are potentially harmful to others near us; and where daily acts of protection and isolation when sick, and masking and vaccination when healthy, are acts of care and responsibility toward one another. What would it mean truly to acknowledge, rather than to deny, this intimate and global intertwinement?[9]

Thinking with Melanie Klein and Judith Butler about mutual dependency and vulnerability, and the disavowal that animates much contemporary politics, seems particularly useful in this moment when we are keenly aware and deeply angered by the incompetence and injustice that made the pandemic as terrible as it has been – by the knowledge that it did not have to be this way if we truly acknowledged the need for mutual care. At the same time, we also know that these are injustices in which we are all implicated as citizens and beneficiaries of structures of global capital, environmental harm, extraction, racism, and inequality.[10]

---

[8] Melanie Klein, *Love, Guilt and Reparation, and other works, 1921*-1945, Delacorte Press, 1975, 306–343. "Love Guilt and Reparation" was first presented as a public lecture in London in March 1936 under the auspices of the Institute of Psycho-Analysis and subsequently published in 1937. But Klein had begun to develop her ideas about reparation in the 1920s. See Meira Likierman, *Melanie Klein: Her Work in Context*, Continuum, 2001, 80.

[9] On intertwinement, a term she borrows from Maurice Merleau-Ponty, see Judith Butler, *What World Is This? A Pandemic Phenomenology*, Columbia University Press, 2022, 106, 107.

[10] Michael Rothberg, *The Implicated Subject: Beyond Victims and Perpetrators*, Stanford University Press, 2019. Bruce Robbins, *The Beneficiary*, Duke University Press, 2017.

How to heal from loss that is compounded by anger and rage, both at ourselves and at others whom we hold responsible? How to accept responsibility for repair?

In our project, my colleagues and I decided to use the term *repair* rather than *reparation*. We see *repair* as a *process* and a *practice* of patching, darning, and mending – as a series of small acts, reiterated and repeated, rather than something, like reparation, that could once and for all be attained or awarded. We can practice repair in the interest of addressing past wrongs and re-envisioning the present and future.[11]

To develop concrete practices of repair, we turned to Bessel van der Kolk's widely read book *The Body Keeps the Score*, originally published in 2014, but only recently a bestseller.[12] Van der Kolk not only shows us how trauma lives in the individual body, but he also maps some roads toward healing that involve embodied practices as shared acts of community building. His decades-long experience treating traumatized patients focused primarily on survivors of war and child sexual abuse and thus his findings do not exactly fit the punctual trauma of pandemic bereavement, compounded by the ongoing debilitating effects of racism, injustice, and inequality that have impacted those who are most vulnerable and affected by Covid 19. And yet, van der Kolk's reflections on the isolating effects of traumatic loss, and on the possible paths toward individual and communal healing, proved helpful in our thinking. We relied especially on his findings that, lodged in the body, trauma cannot be healed through language, or through a talking cure, alone. It involves altering the bodily places where pain lives like a parasitic intruder. *The Body Keeps the Score* investigates the reparative effects of therapeutic techniques ranging from Cognitive Behavioral Therapy and Eye Movement Desensitization and Reprocessing [EMDR], to acupuncture, massage, yoga, performance, and art practices. Some of these practices enable us to do more than to jettison disabling memories, so as to move beyond. They also make it possible to *revise and reconfigure the past*, imagining different paths and possibilities. Describing the process of creating "structures" in which we can relive difficult moments of our past in the company of witnesses who represent and perform characters in our inner lives, van der Kolk writes, "In my experience, physically reexperiencing the past in the present and then reworking it in a safe and supportive 'container' can be powerful

---

[11] On repair, see Marianne Hirsch and Leo Spitzer, "Small Acts of Repair: The Unclaimed Legacy of the Romanian Holocaust," *Journal of Literature and Trauma Studies* 4.1–2 (Spring/Fall, 2015), 13–42; Katherine Franke, *Repair: Redeeming the Promise of Abolition*, Haymarket Books, 2019; Elizabeth V. Spelman, *Repair: The Impulse to Restore in a Fragile World*, Beacon, 2002.
[12] Bessel van der Kolk, *The Body Keeps the Score: Brain, Mind and Body in the Healing of Trauma*, Penguin, 2014.

Figure 3: Acquí/Here Workshop with María José Contreras. Fall 2021, New York City. Photo by Sylvia Juliana RT.

enough to create new supplemental memories: simulated experiences of growing up in an attuned affectionate setting where you are protected from harm."[13] In such a safe theater of memory, we can act out and thus transform disabling memories and the places where these memories sit in our bodies. Together, through acts of mutual care, we can imagine an otherwise. We can transform the very bodies

---

[13] Bessel van der Kolk, *The Body Keeps the Score: Brain, Mind and Body in the Healing of Trauma,* Penguin, 2014, 302.

that hold these memories. It was the aim of the Zip Code Memory Project to create a such a "safe and supportive container" in our communities.

Workshops and gatherings

The project's first two workshops were based on performance exercises, such as those offered by Augusto Boal in his ground-breaking book *Theater of the Oppressed*.[14] These are indeed, as the name of the first workshop run by George Emilio Sanchez, indicates, "Rehearsals for Change" in which participants respond to several initially playful and then increasingly serious prompts to build trust, collectivity, and political awareness, and in which they eventually come to confront their responses to Covid directly.[15] Play and improvisation enable us to unlearn well-worn paths and responses, and to rehearse alternatives. They enable us to be open to surprise. That openness to surprise is especially important in the kind of suspended present we experienced during the first pandemic years with new variants and new lockdowns following unexpectedly on one another. It could help us to survive and transform the shock and rage that emerged in response to continued institutional failure, and to assume responsibility and engage in action rather than passive acceptance. When trauma returns, it intrudes on the present with unaltered frozen fragments from the past. If we rehearse the possibility that the past could have happened differently from the way it happened, we can make space for a future that might be more open-ended.[16] This, in fact, is the meaning of a rehearsal. The workshops rehearsed our Covid present as a time of such openness and a rehearsal for change, rather than a rushing toward a "return" to a previous "normal."

In the second workshop, "Aquí/Here," run by María José Contreras, we built on the scenarios of the first by focusing more closely on our own stories and bodily reactions.[17] Through body-mapping we were invited to draw where Covid and its losses sit in our bodies and to encounter, as Contreras writes, "what our bodies 'hold' that may not be in our conscious mind. The body map is a great ex-

---

14 Augusto Boal, *Theater of the Oppressed*, trans. Charles A. and María Odilia Leal McBride, Theater Communications Group, 1985.
15 https://zcmp.org/3443-2/.
16 See also Pierre Janet's therapeutic suggestion that patients substitute an image of beauty for an intrusive traumatic memory, thus reconnecting a dissociated past back to the present. See the discussion on Janet in Bessel A. van der Kolk, and Onno van der Hart, "The Intrusive Past: The Flexibility of Memory and Engraving of Trauma," *Trauma: Explorations in Memory*, ed. Cathy Caruth, Johns Hopkins University Press, 1995, 151–182.
17 https://zcmp.org/aqui-here/.

ercise to allow the emerging of complex, ambivalent and often contradictory memories."[18] Working on our individual body maps, and discussing each others' in small groups, we started expressing the emotions we had not yet articulated. This set the stage for mapping our various locations and trajectories on neighborhood maps, thus putting our divergent – often Zip Code dependent – stories next to each other. Building a collective narrative of Covid-19 and our city meant acknowledging and respecting differences, while also bridging them in flashes of coming together.

Figure 4: Acquí/Here Workshop with María José Contreras. Fall 2021, New York City. Photo by Desirée Rios.

In the spring of 2022, storytelling workshops conceived collaboratively by Kamal Badhey, Jordan Cruz, Noni Carter, and Carina del Valle Schorske guided participants in writing, spoken word, photography, and collage exercises. These workshops moved from memory and acknowledgement in the form of memorializing spirit cards, to articulations of wishes, desires, and demands for justice and repair. Collaborative writing and creation were key to the design of the workshops and participants' stories and images reverberated with one another to produce a

---

18 https://zcmp.org/aqui-here/.

collectivity and a community built from images and words as they were in the process of being articulated.

We concluded the first project year with "Imagine Repair," a set of performances and an exhibition. The interactive songs, chants, rants, secular sermons, and clanging of pots by Fred Moten, Reverend Billy and the Stop Shopping Choir, Amyra Leon, Imani Uzuri, and others, created a space in which our outrage and anger could give way to hope and joy in our togetherness.[19] These performances and the "Imagine Repair" exhibition were testaments to the power of art to condense, move, inspire, mobilize, and support project participants and a larger public, even during moments of historical catastrophe. The exhibition, located in a chapel of the Cathedral of St. John the Divine, was curated by Isin Önol with Aya Labanieh who invited participants to join in the curatorial process. Two workshops on how to prepare the exhibition and the work on the exhibit itself connected artists from very different neighborhoods, circuits and traditions to each other. With curatorial encouragement and generous inclusivity, these artists searched for forms across multiple media that might convey the responsibility to bear witness to this extraordinary historical moment. They came together to express a collective desire for renewed hope and an aspiration for transformative justice. Their work demonstrated how art practices can produce inclusivity, care, and repair specifically by performing the intertwinement of bodies and the recognition of loss.

Projects made in workshops, such as body maps and spirit cards, were displayed alongside photographs, video, installation art, and animation by artists immediately or more distantly related to the project. Most of the included artists were from neighboring communities or from our team of organizers, but some, like Rafael Lozano-Hemmer and Carrie Mae Weems, generously offered their collaboration with pandemic-related work. Participants were especially interested in creating interactive projects that collected voices and testimonies from the community. For "The Lost New York Covid Story Map," participants Erachie Brown, Yves Dossous, Leah Elimeliah, Yiğit Eygi, and Sonja Jean Killebrew interviewed people in their neighborhoods and edited their voices into a moving collective testimony of pandemic time.[20] "The Depository of Anonymous Feelings 2022," initiated by artist Chelsea Knight with the collaboration of ZCMP participants Sandra Long, Candance Leslie, and Zahied Tony Mohammed, invited New Yorkers to leave one-minute messages on a phone number. These were edited to play on a loop on telephones installed in the gallery.[21]

---

19 https://zcmp.org/imagine-repair-april-may-2022/.
20 https://zcmp.org/kiosk-page/.
21 https://zcmp.org/depository-of-anonymous-feelings-2022/.

Reparative Memory in Practice — **155**

Figure 5: Memorial Altar. Imagine Repair Exhibition, April/May 2022. Photo by Desirée Rios.

Just as the exhibition was in the process of being installed, a group of women from Washington Heights, led by participants Ana-Ofelia Rodriguez, Milagros Batista, and Rafaelina Tineo arrived at the Cathedral with boxes of materials to install an Afro-Dominican altar memorializing the many lives lost to Covid in their community. Young people joined to help and learn these commemorative traditions from their elders. They assembled two altars with paintings of the figure of Yemanja, the Yoruba water spirit, protector and cleanser, syncretized with the Virgin Mary, along with photographs, flowers, embroidery, candles, and drums used in traditional rituals of mourning and remembrance. On the second altar, a series of queer angels made by some of the women to honor their queer children, transformed and re-signified traditional practices to make them more inclusive. The altars became an attraction for the uptown Afro-Dominican community and, at the exhibition closing, drumming, dancing, and song accompanied the altars as they were moved to a new location in Washington Heights when our exhibit closed.

Two of the project's art installations have been ongoing. Through a collaboration with the Brooklyn Museum, visitors to "Imagine Repair" were invited to contribute photographs and stories to Rafael Lozano-Hemmer's digital memorial to those who lost their lives to Covid-19, "A Crack in the Hourglass."[22] And, since the beginning of the exhibition in April 2022, workshop leader María José Contreras has repeated her durational performance "Talk to the Future" in different venues in New York and elsewhere.[23] She invites members of the public to step into a transparent time capsule and to tell her what they want future generations to know about the Covid-19 experience. She then writes phrases from these conversations on the transparent bubble which has been filling up over many months. By means of active listening and sharing in the safe communal container of her time capsule, Contreras allows trauma and grief to shift and transform, if only for a brief moment.

Together, not alone

More than three years after the start of the pandemic, those of us organizing and participating in the Zip Code Memory Project see it as no more than a small and local attempt to grapple with the multiple effects of the pandemic years on a few New York City neighborhoods. But we also hope that it can serve as a space for continuing conversations about imagining repair. Our website meticulously documents and reflects on the process, in itself serving as a kind of publication in the form of a time capsule capturing what this small community could do at a particularly fragile moment. Videos of roundtables, talks, workshops, and events; reflections by project organizers about our key terms; rationales for individual workshops and downloadable tool kits – these are more than a record. They can serve as a syllabus or curriculum for related initiatives, to be adapted to specific needs in different locations. Filmmakers Gabriella Canal and Judith Helfand also made a 20-minute documentary film, *Together, Not Alone* which, in the second year of the project, served as a springboard for showings and discussions in museums, community centers, hostels, and colleges across New York City boroughs. A number of these showings included short films, art projects, and activist initiatives produced in other neighborhoods, thus expanding the conversation.

Many questions remain. As we envisioned this project, we linked "repair" to "justice" and that term proved more difficult to circumscribe. We began by thinking of justice in juridical and political terms and we continue to ask ourselves whether the exercises of the Zip Code Memory Project can enjoin us, in Anne Cheng's terms, to move from grief to grievance, or, in the words of Douglas

---

[22] https://memorialcovid-lozano-hemmer.web.app/?lang=en.
[23] https://zcmp.org/talk-to-the-future/.

Figure 6: "Talk to the Future." Durational performance by María José Contreras. Museum of the City of New York, Spring 2023. Photo by Sylvia Juliana RT.

Crimp, from mourning to militancy. Can practices of reparative memory become springboards for political action?

At an event held at the Museum of the City of New York in February 2023, for example, we asked attendees to fill out postcards responding to the prompts "What Have We Learned?" and "Can We Do Better?" Responses were beautiful and moving. Some had direct policy implications: "Direct public funding to health programs, research and education." "Invest in better ventilation in schools, nursing homes and housing." "Help participants take what we learned to our communities." Other messages were more inward community-directed: "We should try to know and value the people around us." "Doing better means showing up, speaking up, caring for each other authentically." "There is always room for more kindness and empathy."

Showing up, trying to know, caring – these in themselves became modest practices of repair in the wake of the pandemic. I have come to think of them also as practices of justice viewed through the frame of "transformative activism" devised by our collaborator and co-editor of *Women Mobilizing Memory* Ayşe Gül Altinay and her feminist colleagues in Turkey. They describe transformative activism as "an alternative to community building or political organizing practices where conflict, polarization and judgment have become the norm, and to academic and activist practices that put the mind and thinking at centre stage, leaving out the body, emotions and desires."[24] Instead, they suggest practices that take the body and emotions into account. They support political activists through "a coming together where healing happens." In Turkey, the "Transformative Activism" project is geared to feminist and LGBTQIA+ activist communities, a mostly like-minded, though of course not conflict-free, group. And yet, in this very different New York configuration, we also found in the Zip Code Memory Project, a "togetherness that is open to possibilities, surprises, play, dance, song, poetry and endless discoveries and adventures."[25] We continue to hope that as a first step towards emotional recovery, a caring and healing environment that fosters acts of embodied testimony and witness can become a platform for social transformation. Perhaps, in Judith Butler's terms, gatherings such as those we organized are a way to think about how we might "repair forward" allowing "a new imaginary [to] emerge from the hauntings of the present, the liminal horizon of this world."[26]

And yet, justice can be linked to memory in different ways as well. Historian Yosef Yerushalmi ends his book *Zakhor* with reflections about collective forgetting. Citing the projected trial of Klaus Barbie in France, and the survey of the French public on whether the trial should take place in view of the painful memories it would bring up, Yerushalmi provocatively asks: "Is it possible that the antonym of 'forgetting' is not 'remembering,' but *justice*?"[27] He asks this in the context of defining a collective memory that will help those in the future to "find that this person did live, those events really took place, this interpretation is not the only one." Remembering in community thus in itself becomes a form of justice.

And yet, communities of memory such as the ones we formed for the Zip Code Memory Project are as tenuous and fragile as the pronouns that refer to them. Throughout this essay I have been using the pronoun "we" to refer to the five project organizers, (and at times just to the two co-directors), to a very diverse group of project participants, and sometimes in more general terms to those who lived through the pandemic. I need to emphasize here that I say "we," even while knowing that there are many voices, lives, and losses that go into that "we" – none of them the same. These hesitations are similar to the ones the poet and theorist Fred Moten voiced in his presentation at our exhibition opening: "I want to say [we] so badly I can taste it, or smell it, or hear it as if it were being whispered in

---

24 Ebru Nihan Celka, Özge Ertem, Sema Semih, Ayşe Gül Altinay, eds., *From Hand to Hand: Transformative Activism Stories*, Sabanci University, 2022, unnumbered pages.
25 Celka et al., *From Hand to Hand.*
26 *What World Is This?* 99.
27 Yosef Yerushalmi, *Zakhor: Jewish History and Jewish Memory*, University of Washington Press, 1996, e-book, 2011, 117.

my ear. Do I have to earn that right? Will you grant it to me? . . . I feel like I feel something with you, even if it can't be what you feel."[28] As Butler puts it, "loss has made a tenuous 'we' of us all. And 'we' is also 'aspirational.'"[29]

I would like to think of the "we" as anticipatory as well as aspirational, in Butler's terms, as "a way of hoping for a we that does not yet exist." Then, under the right circumstances, that work of aspiring to a tenuous "we," of trying to "earn" it so that it will be "granted," could be the occasion for a new start. It could be a portal to imagining, together, a communal practice of responsibility and repair in a time out of joint.

---

28 https://zcmp.org/together-not-alone/.
29 *What World Is This?* 80.

Appendices

Appendix One

List of Topics and Participants in Conversation Series "Humanities for Humans"

Inaugural Season 2022–2023

"Racism and Fascism: A Love Story"
Michael G. Hanchard, University of Pennsylvania, Africana Studies, Political Science
Dagmar Herzog, City University of New York Graduate School, History, Social Welfare, Women's and Gender Studies
September 27, 2022, in person at 1014: Space for Ideas (Fifth Avenue, New York, New York)

"Imagining Anew the Future of the Earth"
Harriet Hawkins, Royal Holloway, University of London, Geohumanities
Rebecca Tsosie, University of Arizona, Law, Philosophy, Indigenous Studies
December 8, 2022, online

"Systemic Inequalities: Is Change Possible?"
Robin D. G. Kelley, University of California at Los Angeles, History
Bruce Robbins, Columbia University, Humanities, English and Comparative Literature
March 9, 2023, online

"Repair, Reparation, Refusal"
Marianne Hirsch, Columbia University, Comparative Literature, Women's and Gender Studies
Hortense Spillers, Vanderbilt University, English
May 9, 2023, in person at 1014: Space for Ideas (Fifth Avenue, New York, New York)

Season Two 2023–2024

"Gender, Desire, Embodiment"
Meg Fernandes, Poet, and Adjunct Professor and Writer-in-Residence, Lafayette College
Jack Halberstam, Columbia University, Gender Studies and English
October 18, 2023, in person at 1014: Space for Ideas (Fifth Avenue, New York, New York)

"World on the Move"
Kathryn Abrams, University of California at Berkeley, Legal Scholar and Professor
Mark Terkessidis, Berlin, Germany, Independent Scholar
December 7, 2023, online

"Controversy as a Tool for Connection"
Liz Lerman, Choreographer, Teacher, Writer
Martha Minow, Harvard University, Legal Scholar and Professor
February 21, 2024, online

"Organized Religion, Religious Hate, and the Future of Secular Societies"
Susannah Heschel, Dartmouth College, Religion and Jewish Studies
Terrence Johnson, Harvard Divinity School
May 6, 2024, in person at 1014: Space for Ideas (Fifth Avenue, New York, New York)
**this event was postponed and eventually took place on October 15, 2024 online; please see Kacandes's introduction for more information

Appendix Two

Board of Advisors: "Humanities for Humans"

Jennifer F. Hamer, Penn State University
Professor of African American Studies and Women's, Gender, and Sexuality Studies
Senior Faculty Mentor, Office of the Vice Provost for Educational Equity
Ph.D. in Sociology, University of Texas at Austin

Michael P. McDonald, University of Florida
Professor of Political Science
Ph.D. in Political Science, University of California at San Diego

Helmut Walser Smith, Vanderbilt University
Martha Rivers Ingram Professor of History
Ph.D. in History, Yale University

John H. McWhorter, Columbia University
Ph.D. in Linguistics, Stanford University

Manuela Gerlof, De Gruyter Foundation
Chief Publishing Officer, De Gruyter Brill
Ph.D. in German Literature, Humboldt University Berlin

Katja Wiesbrock Donovan, 1014
Executive Director 1014
Ph.D. in International Law, University of Göttingen

Irene Kacandes, Dartmouth College, 1014 Board Member, De Gruyter book series editor
The Dartmouth Professor of German Studies and Comparative Literature
Ph.D. in Comparative Literature, Harvard University

Appendix Three

Readings on topics covered in Seasons One and Two of "Humanities for Humans." The names of speakers in the original conversations are indicated with bold type.

Racism, fascism, inequality

Literature

Michelle Alexander, *The New Jim Crow: Mass Incarceration in the Age of Colorblindness*. 10th Anniversary Edition. The New Press, 2020.
Natalie Angier, "Do Races Differ? Not Really, DNA Shows." Science Section, *NYT*, August 22, 2000.
Kathleen Belew and Ramón A. Gutiérrez, eds., *A Field Guide to White Supremacy*. University of California Press, 2021.
Cristina Beltrán, *Cruelty as Citizenship: How Migrant Suffering Sustains White Democracy*. Forerunners: Ideas First series, 2020.
Anne Berg, *Empire of Rags and Bones: Waste and War in Nazi Germany*. Oxford University Press, 2024.
Doris Bergen, *War and Genocide: A Concise History of the Holocaust*. Rowman and Littlefield, 2016 edition.
The Black Public Sphere Collective, ed., *The Black Public Sphere (Series): A Public Culture Book (Black Literature and Culture)*. University of Chicago Press Journals, 1995.
Silvia Federici, "Feminism and the Politics of the Commons" online in *The Commoner* (2011). https://thecommoner.org/wp-content/uploads/2020/06/federici-feminism-and-the-politics-of-commons.pdf.
Barbara J. Fields and Karen E. Fields, *Racecraft: The Soul of Inequality in American Life*. Verso, 2022.
David Graeber and David Wengrow, *The Dawn of Everything: A New History of Humanity*. Farrar, Straus and Giroux, 2021, esp. chapters 1 and 2.
Raphael Gross, "Guilt, Shame, Anger, Indignation: Nazi Law and Nazi Morals," in Alan E. Steinweis and Robert D. Rachlin, eds., *The Law in Nazi Germany: Ideology, Opportunism, and the Perversion of Justice*. Berghahn, 2013, 88–103.
Stuart Hall, *The Fateful Triangle: Race, Ethnicity, Nation. The W. E. B. Du Bois Lectures*. Edited and introduced by Kobena Mercer. With a Foreword by Henry Louis Gates, Jr. Unabridged Edition. Harvard University Press, 2017.
Michael G. Hanchard, *The Spectre of Race: How Discrimination Haunts Western Democracy*. Princeton University Press, 2018.
Nicole Hannah-Jones, ed., *The 1619 Project*. 2019, 2021 (Originally published by the *New York Times* in its magazine, the contents have been reworked and published as a book, a blog, a TV series, and in a children's version).
Dagmar Herzog, *Sex After Fascism: Memory and Morality in Twentieth-Century Germany*. Princeton University Press, 2007.
Dagmar Herzog, *The Question of Unworthy Life: Eugenics and Germany's Twentieth Century*. Princeton University Press, 2024.
Martha S. Jones, *Vanguard. How Black Women Broke Barriers, Won the Vote, and Insisted on Equality for All*. Basic Books, 2020.

∂ Open Access. © 2025 the author(s), published by De Gruyter. [CC BY-NC-ND] This work is licensed under the Creative Commons Attribution-NonCommercial-NoDerivatives 4.0 International License.
https://doi.org/10.1515/9783111531489-013

Colin Kaepernick, **Robin D. G. Kelley**, and Keeanga-Yamahtta Taylor, eds. *Our History Has Always Been Contraband. In Defense of Black Studies*. Haymarket Books, 2023.

Anthony Kauders, "From Particularism to Mass Murder: Nazi Morality, Antisemitism, and Cognitive Dissonance," *Holocaust and Genocide Studies* 36, no. 1 (Spring 2022): 46–59.

Robin D. G. Kelley, *Yo' Mama's DisFunktional! Fighting the Culture Wars in Urban America*. Beacon, 1997.

Robin D. G. Kelley, *Freedom Dreams: Twentieth Anniversary Edition: The Black Radical Imagination*. Beacon, 2022.

Darrin M. McMahon, *Equality: The History of An Elusive Idea*. Basic Books, 2023.

Angela Marshall and Kathy Palakoff, *Dismissed: Tackling the Biases that Undermine our Health Care*. Citadel, 2023.

Branko Milanovic, *Global Inequality: A New Approach for the Age of Globalization*. Belknap, 2018.

Branko Milanovic, *The Haves and the Have-Nots: A Brief and Idiosyncratic History of Global Inequality*. Reprint edition. Basic Books, 2012.

Jennifer L. Morgan, *Reckoning with Slavery: Gender, Kinship, and Capitalism in the Early Black Atlantic*. Duke University Press, 2021.

Robert O. Paxton, *The Anatomy of Fascism*. Vintage, 2004.

David O. Pendas, Mark Roseman, and Richard F. Wetzell, eds. *Beyond the Racial State: Rethinking Nazi Germany*. Cambridge University Press, 2017.

Vishad Prashad, *The Poorer Nations: A Possible History of the Global South*. Verso, 2012.

Adolph Reed, Jr., *Class Notes: Posing as Politics and Other Thoughts on the American Scene*, New Press, 2001, especially the chapter called "Token Equality." https://www.thefreelibrary.com/Token+equality.-a019056324.

Bruce Robbins, *The Beneficiary*. Duke University Press, 2017.

Bruce Robbins, *Upward Mobility and the Common Good: Toward a Literary History of the Welfare State*. Princeton University Press, 2009.

Walter Rodney, *How Europe Underdeveloped Africa*. Verso, 2018, orig. 1972.

Adam Serwer, *The Cruelty Is the Point: Why Trump's America Endures*. One World, 2021.

Joseph P. Shapiro, *No Pity: People with Disabilities Forging a New Civil Rights Movement*. Three Rivers, 1994. Read helpfully in tandem with the memoir *Being Heumann: An Unrepentant Memoir of a Disabilities Rights Activist* by Judith Heumann. Beacon, 2021.

Timothy Snyder, "The War on History is a War on Democracy." *NYT Sunday Magazine*, June 29, 2021.

Michael E. Staub, *The Mismeasure of Minds. Debating Race and Intelligence Between Brown and The Bell Curve*. University of North Carolina Press, 2018.

Keeanga-Yamahtta Taylor, ed. *How We Get Free: Black Feminism and the Combahee River Collective*. Haymarket Books, 2017.

Keeanga-Yamahtta Taylor, *Race for Profit: How Banks and the Real Estate Industry Undermined Black Homeownership*. University of North Carolina Press, 2021.

Alberto Toscano, *Late Fascism: Race, Capitalism, and the Politics of Crisis*. Verso, 2023.

Enzo Traverso, *The New Faces of Fascism: Populism and the Far Right*. Verso, 2019.

James Q. Whitman, *Hitler's American Model: The United States and the Making of Nazi Race Law*. Princeton University Press, 2017.

Richard G. Wilkinson and Kate Pickett, *The Spirit Level: Why Greater Equality Makes Societies Stronger*. Bloomsbury, 2011.

Audio-visual material

Mudbound, film, dir. Dee Rees, 2017.
Phoenix, film, dir. Christian Petzold, 2014.
Small Axe. A Collection of Five Films, film, written and dir. Steve McQueen, 2020.
The Underground Railroad, mini-series, dir. Barry Jenkins, 2021, or the novel of same title by Colson Whitehead, 2016.

Reparation, repair, refusal

Literature

General
Elizabeth Alexander, *The Trayvon Generation*. Grand Central Publishing, 2022.

Marianne Hirsch, *The Generation of Postmemory: Writing and Visual Culture after the Holocaust*. Columbia University Press, 2021.

Marianne Hirsch et al., "The Zip Code Memory Project: Practices of Justice and Repair." https://zcmp.org.

Marianne Hirsch, "Acts of Memory and Repair in a Suspended Present: New York City 2022." https://zcmp.org/resources/.

Irene Kacandes, ed., *On Being Adjacent to Historical Violence*. De Gruyter, 2022.

Martha Minow, *Between Vengeance and Forgiveness: Facing History After Genocide and Mass Violence*. Beacon, 1999.

Hortense Spillers, *Black, White, and In Color: Essays on American Literature and Culture*. University of Chicago Press, 2003.

Hortense Spillers, "Afro Pessimism and Its Others." https://event.newschool.edu/ICSIHortenseSpillers.

Linda Villarosa, *Under the Skin: The Hidden Toll of Racism*. Doubleday, 2022.

Bessel A. van der Kolk, *The Body Keeps the Score: Brain, Mind, and Body in the Healing of Trauma*. Penguin, 2014.

Repair
Judith Lewis Herman, *Truth and Repair: How Trauma Survivors Envision Justice*. Basic, 2023.

Elizabeth Spelman, *Repair: The Impulse to Restore in a Fragile World*. Beacon, 2003.

Reparation
Ta-Nehisi Coates, "The Case for Reparations." https://www.theatlantic.com/magazine/archive/2014/06/the-case-for-reparations/361631/.

William A. Darity Jr. and A. Kirsten Mullen, *From Here to Equality: Reparations for Black Americans in the Twenty-First Century*. 2nd ed. University of North Carolina Press, 2022.

N. Bruce Duthu, *American Indians and the Law*. Penguin 2008, 2009.

Katherine Franke, *Repair: Redeeming the Promise of Abolition*. 2nd ed. Haymarket Books, 2021.

Susan Neiman, *Learning from the Germans: Race and the Memory of Evil*. Picador, 2020.

Susan Slyomovics, *How to Accept German Reparations*. University of Pennsylvania Press, 2014.

Craig Steven Wilder, *Ebony and Ivy: Race, Slavery, and the Troubled History of America's Universities*. Bloomsbury, 2013.

Refusal
Tina Campt, *A Black Gaze: Artists Changing How We See*. MIT University Press, 2021.

Saidiya Hartman, *Wayward Lives, Beautiful Experiments: Intimate Histories of Riotous Black Girls, Troublesome Women, and Queer Radicals*. Norton, 2020.

Bonnie Honig, *A Feminist Theory of Refusal*. Harvard University Press, 2021.
Christina Sharpe, *Ordinary Notes*. Farrar, Straus, Giroux, 2023.
Audra Simpson, *Mohawk Interruptus: Political Life Across the Borders of Settler States*. Duke University Press, 2014.

The irreparable
Robin Blaser, "The Irreparable," in Miriam Nichols, ed., *The Fire: Collected Essays of Robin Blaser*. University of California Press, 2006.
Eva Rieter, *Preventing Irreparable Harm: Provisional Measures in International Human Rights Adjudication*. Intersentia, 2010.

Audio-visual material

Hortense Spillers, "Shades of Intimacy: What the Eighteenth-Century Teaches Us." Gates Lecture 2016. Department of African American Studies, Yale University. Recording. https://afamstudies.yale.edu/media-gallery/gates-lecture-2016-hortense-spillers.

Turning controversy into connection

Literature

David Brooks, *How to Know a Person: The Art of Seeing Others Deeply and Being Deeply Seen*. Random House, 2023.

Tina Campt, *A Black Gaze: Artists Changing How We See*. MIT University Press, 2021.

Facing History and Ourselves, *The Reconstruction Era and Fragility of Democracy*. https://www.facinghistory.org/resource-library/reconstruction-era-and-fragility-democracy-0.

Judith Lewis Herman, *Truth and Repair: How Trauma Survivors Envision Justice*. Basic, 2023.

Irene Kacandes, ed. *On Being Adjacent to Historical Violence*. De Gruyter, 2022.

Liz Lerman, *Critique is Creative*. Wesleyan Press, 2022.

Liz Lerman, *Liz Lerman's Critical Response Process*. Liz Lerman Dance Exchange, 2003.

Liz Lerman, CRP One Pager. https://acrobat.adobe.com/link/track?uri=urn%3Aaaid%3Ascds%3AUS%3A05c47fa7-0974-4f0f-bd03-f6f2fcb91c0f&viewer%21megaVerb=group-discover.

Liz Lerman, *Hiking the Horizontal: Field Notes from a Choreographer*. Wesleyan University Press, 2011.

Liz Lerman, "Small Dances About Big Ideas" (at Harvard Law School in Commemoration of 60th Anniversary of the Nuremberg Trials; in consultation with Martha Minow). https://lizlerman.com/2018/05/17/small-dances-about-big-ideas/.

Liz Lerman. Website. https://lizlerman.com.

Martha Minow, *Between Vengeance and Forgiveness: Facing History After Genocide and Mass Violence*. Beacon, 1999.

Martha Minow, *When Should Law Forgive?* Norton, 2019.

Martha Minow, "Walls or Bridges: Law's Role in Conflicts over Religion and Equal Treatment," 48 *Brigham Young L. Rev.* 1581 (2023), https://digitalcommons.law.byu.edu/lawreview/vol48/iss5/7/.

Martha Minow, "Learning How to Forgive," *Criminal* (Podcast May 1, 2020), https://thisiscriminal.com/episode-139-learning-how-to-forgive-5-1-2020/.

Martha Minow, "Can Americans Forgive One Another," *Project Syndicate* (December 21, 2020). https://www.project-syndicate.org/commentary/what-a-politically-divided-america-should-prioritize-by-martha-minow-2020-12.

Martha Minow, "Respectfully resolving tensions between religion, law is possible," with Michael McConnell, *Boston Globe*, May 27, 2015. https://www.bostonglobe.com/opinion/2015/05/27/respectfully-resolvingtensions-between-religion-law-possible/IRgR30PYQYSgCDrp2USpBP/story.html#.

Martha Minow, "Turning Conflict into Connection." https://www.thenationalcouncil.org/wp-content/uploads/2021/09/Turning-Conflict-Into-Connection.pdf.

Elaine Scarry, *Thinking in an Emergency*. W.W. Norton & Company, 2011.

Christina Sharpe, *Ordinary Notes*. Farrar, Straus, Giroux, 2023.

Elizabeth Spelman, *Repair: The Impulse to Restore in a Fragile World*. Beacon 2003.

Douglas Stone, Bruce Patton, Sheila Heen (of the Harvard Negotiation Project), *Difficult Conversations: How to Discuss What Matters Most*. Revised ed. Penguin, 2023.

Isabel Wilkerson, *Caste. The Origins of Our Discontents*. Random House, 2020.

Audio-visual material

Amerikatsi, written and dir. Michael A. Goorjian, 2023.
Origin, dir. Ava DuVernay, 2023.
The Promised Land, dir. Nikolaj Arcel and written by Nicolaj Arcel and Anders Thomas Jensen, 2023.
"What Relationships Would You Want if You Believed They were Possible?"
With Rhaina Cohen, The Ezra Klein Show, 6 Feb 2024. Podcast.
https://www.nytimes.com/2024/02/06/opinion/ezra-klein-podcast-rhaina-cohen.html.

Climate change

Literature

Randall S. Abate and Elizabeth Ann Kronk, eds., *Climate Change and Indigenous Peoples: The Search for Legal Remedies*. Edward Elgar Publishers, 2013.

Lawrence Buell, *The Environmental Imagination: Thoreau, Nature Writing, and the Formation of American Culture*. Harvard University Press, 1996.

Basil Camu, *From Wasteland to Wonder: Easy Ways We Can Help Heal Earth in the Sub/Urban Landscape*. Leaf and Limb, 2024.

Alenda Chang, *Playing Nature: Ecology in Video Games*. University of Minnesota Press, 2019.

David Farrier, *Anthropocene Poetics: Deep Time, Sacrifice Zones and Extinction*. University of Minnesota Press, 2019.

Macarena Gomez-Barris, *The Extractive Zone. Social Ecologies and Decolonial Perspectives*. Duke University Press, 2017.

Harriet Hawkins and AM Kanngieser, "Artful climate change communication: overcoming abstractions, insensibilities, and distances," *WIREs Climate Change* 8: e472 (2017).

Harriet Hawkins, Sallie A. Marston, Mrill Ingram and Elizabeth Straughan, "The Arts of Socio-Ecological Transformation." *Annals of the Association of American Geographers* 105.2 (2015): 331–341.

Mike Hulme ed., *Climates and Cultures*. 6 vols. Sage Publications Ltd., 2015.

Adeline Johns-Putra, "Climate change in literature and literary studies: From cli-fi, climate change theater and ecopoetry to ecocriticism and climate change criticism." *WIREs Clim Change* 7 (2016): 266–282.

Robin Wall Kimmerer, *Braiding Sweetgrass: Indigenous Wisdom, Scientific Knowledge, and the Teachings of Plants*. Milkweed Editions, 2013.

Abrahm Lustgarten, *On the Move: The Overheating of the Earth and the Uprooting of America*. Farrar, Straus and Giroux, 2024.

Jessica May and Marshall N. Price, *Second Nature: Photography in the Age of the Anthropocene*. Rizzoli Electa, 2024.

Malcolm Miles, *Eco-Aesthetics: Art, Literature and Architecture in a Period of Climate Change*. Bloomsbury, 2024.

Kathleen Dean Moore and Michael P. Nelson, eds., *Moral Ground: Ethical Action for a Planet in Peril*. Trinity University Press, 2010.

Melissa K. Nelson and Dan Shilling, eds., *Traditional Ecological Knowledge: Learning from Indigenous Practices for Environmental Sustainability*. Cambridge University Press, 2018.

Richard Powers, *The Overstory*. Norton, 2018.

Kate Rigby, *Dancing with Disaster: Environmental Histories, Narratives and Ethics for Perilous Times*. University of Virginia Press, 2015.

Kim Stanley Robinson, *Ministry for the Future: A Novel*. Orbit, 2020.

Vandana Shiva, *Making Peace with the Earth*. Pluto Press, 2013.

Jeff Speck, *Walkable City: How Downtown Can Save America, One Step at a Time*. 10th Anniversary Edition. Picador Paper, 2022.

Rebecca Tsosie, "Indigenous People and Environmental Justice: The Impact of Climate Change," *Colorado Law Review* 78 (2007): 1625–1677.

Arts organizations

Cape Farewell. https://www.capefarewell.com.
Arts Catalyst. https://artscatalyst.org.

Migration

Literature

Kathryn Abrams, *Open Hand, Closed Fist. Practices of Undocumented Organizing in a Hostile State*. University of California Press, 2022.
Jason De León, *Soldiers and Kings: Survival and Hope in the World of Human Smuggling*. Viking, 2024.
Kaitlin Dickerson, "The Secret History of the U.S. Government's Family Separation Policy." *The Atlantic*, August 7, 2022.
Elena Fiddian-Qasmiyeh, Gil Loescher, Katy Long, Sigona Nando, eds., *The Oxford Handbook of Refugee and Forced Migration Studies*. Oxford University Press, 2014.
Claudia Finotelli and Irene Ponzo, eds., "Introduction: Understanding Migration Controls in Europe," in *Migration Control Logics and Strategies in Europe: A North-South Comparison*. https://doi.org/10.1007/978-3-031-26002-5_1.
Roberto Gonzales, *Lives in Limbo: Undocumented and Coming of Age in America*. University of California Press, 2015.
Gil Loescher, *Refugees: A Very Short Introduction*. Oxford University Press, 2021.
Ana Raquel Minian, *In the Shadow of Liberty. The Invisible History of Immigrant Detention in the United States*. Viking, 2024.
Movements Journal. https://movements-journal.org.
Maxi Obexer, *No Man's Land* (orig. title: *Illegale Helfer* [Illegal Helpers], orig. pub. 2015). Eng. trans. by Neil Blackadder. Published online by New German Literature in English. https://www.no-mans-land.org/article/illegal-helpers/.
Patrice Poutrus, *Umkämpftes Asyl: Vom Nachkriegsdeutschland bis in die Gegenwart* [Contested Asylum: From Postwar Germany to the Present]. Ch. Links, 2019.
Ayelet Shachar, *The Birthright Lottery: Citizenship and Global Inequality*. Harvard University Press, 2009.
Ayelet Shachar (in dialog with others), *The Shifting Border: Legal Cartographies of Migration and Mobility*. Manchester University Press, 2020.
Mark Terkessidis, "Migrants and Tourists: The Similarities between Travel for Pleasure and Travel out of Necessity." *Art & Thought/Fikrun wa Fann*. N.d.: 12–15.
Mark Terkessidis, *Nach der Flucht. Neue Ideen für die Einwanderungsgesellschaft* [After Flight. New Ideas for the Immigration Society]. Reclam, 2017.

Audio-visual material

Lacie Heeley and Katie Toth, "Belarus-Poland Border Wall is Impacting Refugees and Wildlife." Originally broadcast on *The World*, Wednesday, November 29, 2023. Podcast. https://theworld.org/segments/2024/04/04/belarus-poland-border-wall-is-impacting-refugees-and-wildlife.
Flee, film, dir. Jonas Poher Rasmussen, 2021.
Green Border (*Zielona granica*), film, dir. Agnieszka Holland, 2023.
Winter in Lampedusa, film, dir. Jakob Brossmann, 2015.

Further reading

Benedict Anderson, *Imagined Communities: Reflection on the Origin and Spread of Nationalism*. Verso, 2006 (orig. pub. 1983).

Didier Fassin, *Deepening Divides: How Territorial Borders and Social Boundaries Delineate Our World*. Pluto Press, 2020.

Welcome to the United States. A Guide for New Immigrants. Authored and published by the United States Citizenship and Immigration Services, 2022.

Gender and desire

General

Miliann Kang, Donovan Lessard, Laura Heston, Sonny Nordmarken, *Introduction to Women, Gender, Sexuality Studies*. University of Massachusetts, Amherst. Open Textbook Library, 2017.

Literature

Judith Butler, *Who's Afraid of Gender?* MacMillan, 2024.
Don Kulick, "The Gender of Brazilian Transgendered Prostitutes," originally appeared in *American Anthropologist* 99/3 (1997): 574–584. Can also be found in the great anthology *The Masculinities Studies Reader* (2002), eds. Rachel Adams and David Savran.
Audre Lorde, "Age, Race, Class, Sex," *Sister Outsider*. Crossing Press, Random House, 1984, 2007.
Audre Lorde, *Zami, A New Spelling of My Name. A Biomythography*, Crossing Press, 1982.

Selected publications by our experts

Meg Fernandes, *I Do Everything I'm Told. Poems*. Tin House, 2023.
Meg Fernandes, *Good Boys. Poems*. Tin House, 2020.
Meg Fernandes, *The Kingdom and After*. Tightrope Books, 2015.

Jack Halberstam, *Wild Things: The Disorder of Desire*. Duke University Press, 2020.
Jack Halberstam, *Trans*: A Quick and Quirky Account of Gender Variability*. Beacon, 2012.
Jack Halberstam, *The Queer Art of Failure*. Duke University Press, 2011.

Audio-visual material

"We Need Better Narratives About Gender," a conversation between Masha Gessen and Lydia Polgreen on the Ezra Klein Show, October 10, 2023. Podcast. https://www.nytimes.com/2023/10/10/opinion/ezra-klein-podcast-masha-gessen-oct-2023.html.
Judith Butler, *Who's Afraid of Gender?* Judith Butler's public lecture at University of Cambridge 2023, sponsored by Q+@cam. Recording. https://www.youtube.com/watch?v=yD6UukSbAMs.

Further reading

José Esteban Muñoz, "Introduction: Feeling Utopia," *Cruising Utopia: The Then and There of Queer Futurity*. New York University Press, 2009, 1–18.

Jennifer Christine Nash, "Intersectionality and Its Discontents," *American Quarterly* 69.1 (2017): 117–129.
Maggie Nelson, *The Argonauts*. Graywolf Press, 2016.
Paul Preciado, *Testo-Junkie: Sex, Drugs and Biopolitics in the Pharmacopornographic Era* (English trans., The Feminist Press, 2013; first published in French and Spanish 2008)
Jordy Rosenberg, *Confessions of the Fox: A Novel*. Random House, 2018.
Riley Snorton, *Black on Both Sides: A Racial History of Trans Identity*. University of Minnesota Press, 2018.
Dean Spade, "For Lovers and Fighters," in Melody Berger, ed., *We Don't Need Another Wave: Dispatches from the Next Generation of Feminists*. Seal Press, 2006.
Dean Spade, "Mutilating Gender" in Susan Stryker and Stephen Whittle, eds., *The Transgender Studies Reader*, Vol. I. Routledge, 2006.
Alice Wong, ed., *Disability Intimacy: Essays on Love, Care, and Desire*. Vintage, 2024.

Queer poetry recommended by Meg Fernandes

KB Brookins, *Freedom House*. Deep Vellum, 2023.
Jameson Fitzpatrick, *Pricks in the Tapestry*. Birds, 2020.
Taylor Johnson, *Inheritance*. Alice James Books, 2020.
Maggie Millner, *Couplets: A Love Story*. Farrar, Straus, Giroux, 2023.
Jay Gao, *Imperium*. Carcaret, 2022.

Films

(very short selection; there's a lot out there)

Bigger on the Inside, film, dir. Angelo Madsen Minax, 2022 (recommended by Meg Fernandes)
Chicken Run, film, dir. Peter Lord, Nick Park, 2000 (recommended by Jack Halberstam)
Girl, film, dir. Lukas Dhant, 2018 (recommended by Irene Kacandes)

More?

The New York Public Library has put together an extensive list on "Trans and Nonbinary Reads for Adults" that can be found at:
https://www.nypl.org/books-more/recommendations/trans-reads/adults.

www.ingramcontent.com/pod-product-compliance
Lightning Source LLC
Chambersburg PA
CBHW061716300426
44115CB00014B/2707